SO WHAT DO I KNOW

CONFESSIONS OF A MID-LIFE
DOG GROOMER

Written by Georgeanne Hoffman

SO WHAT DO I KNOW

COMMONLY ASKED QUESTIONS ON DOG OWNERSHIP

Written by Georgeanne Hoffman

Edited by Kelly O'Connor McNees and Antoinette Frazho
Illustrated by Matthew D. Malcangi
Cover by Matthew D. Malcangi
Back Cover by Resa Malcangi

ISBN 978-0-615-29968-6

Published by: Geo Publishing, LLC
                     P.O. Box 410
                     Dewitt, MI 48820
                     www.so-what-do-i-know.com

To err is **HUMAN**

to forgive, CANINE

ACKNOWLEDGMENTS

I would like to thank all the wonderful people who have entrusted their family members (pets) to me for so many years. Their dedication and loyalty allowed me to learn, grow, and absorb much of what is detailed in this book.

My deepest appreciation to my loyal friend, Antoinette, for many hours of typing my hen-scratched writing.

A big thank you to Vicki for the perfect subtitle.

With deep gratitude and pride, to my nephew, Matt, for all the hours spent developing the artwork throughout the book.

To my sister, Resa, for her wit in helping with the back cover.

To Melanie Williams, a huge thank you for graphics and web design.

To Pat Fortino at writenowdesign.com, who programmed and established my web page, truly making it a virtual reality.

Big hugs to friends and family for taking the time to add their thoughts and ideas in review of my lifelong occupational masterpiece.

Lastly, to all those who helped me polish it for your reading pleasure.

I wish you many years of enjoyment,
Georgeanne Hoffman

INTRODUCTION

As a young girl, my passion for any kind of animal to touch, hug, or drag home was very strong. It was extremely easy for me to find all kinds of so-called homeless dogs and walk them home to our house. As I got older, the passion grew and in my late teens I started down what is now a thirty-five-plus-year journey with dogs and their wonderful owners. Having an occupation as a dog groomer for what is a collection of decades, I have, as any professional does, become very attuned to dogs and their bodies. I gathered information and methods of treatment through the hundreds of dogs I have had the privilege to know. Producing a book containing all the hints I had in my bag of tricks never really occurred to me until one day in my early fifties, I started that mid-life soul searching and decided to give it a shot. All I can say is thank God for spell check. So here I am, offering this A to Z helpful hints volume for you to enjoy and possibly find useful in many ways. I want you to learn, laugh, and finally love all the reasons you decided to own a dog. This book was written as a kind of recipe book to answer the immediate issue at hand and with references for further information. I encourage you to read as many books on the subject as you can get your hands on, for that is the true method of learning.

So What Do I Know is not a so-called medical book for dogs; however, it does cover many of the run-of-the-mill medical issues that crop up when owning a dog. The advice I give is solely the personal solutions I have found helpful in many of the real-life dog scenarios I have experienced. Having the ability to regularly revisit situations in monthly and bimonthly appointments has allowed me to gather different ideas for dealing with the most common dog owner events. My goal is to offer the best common-sense approaches to save you time and money. I sincerely hope you enjoy this book and send my deepest appreciation to you for reading it.

I want the readers to know that the information I am providing in this book does not replace nor supersede the advice and guidance of your veterinarian. I'm not a veterinarian and only seek to offer my personal advice based on years of caring for dogs. If your beloved pet does not agree with the advice provided in this book, please seek the advice of a professional. This book offers a possible solution, but not the only one.

WELCOME!

Table of Contents

Abscess	Anal Glands
Accidents	Anxiety
Acne	Arthritis
Adoption	Aspirin
Aging	
Aggressive Behavior	
Allergies	

"Appreciate" - it's my sincere hope that you always appreciate and recognize the value of your relationship to each other. Man and dog.

Abscess - An abscess is usually caused by a puncture from an animal bite that seals bacteria under the skin, causing it to grow like crazy. Punctures are bad news because most pet owners are not aware that any infection is cultivating until the dog is quite ill. If you know that your dog has been in a tussle and you think this injury is just a small mark, think again. These "little marks" can end up becoming a huge ordeal. Carefully cut the hair away from the wound, clean the area with peroxide, and fill the hole with triple antibiotic cream. You also need to get your dog to the veterinarian for antibiotics. An abscess can take several days to form, so keep a watchful eye on the damaged area. Hot compresses with Epsom salts always help.

Accidents - If we have pets, there are bound to be accidents at some point. There is a good chance that Murphy's Law will come knocking at the most inappropriate time. Be prepared with a First Aid Kit and phone numbers. Know where your after-hours clinics are and how to get there along with your own veterinarian. Accidents are high-stress moments. Try to remain in control and get to where you need to go safely.
See - First Aid Kit

Acne - Many dogs get acne on their faces and bellies. This acne is usually red in appearance, like human pimples with white heads. Acne can be treated by your veterinarian with great success. I find acne occurs a lot in the spring and summer months. Also, if you have a breed with thick hair, i.e., Cocker Spaniel, have the hair cut short to help in the healing process. Change to stainless steel bowls instead of plastic, because stainless steel cannot harbor bacteria. Short-haired bulldog types also seem to be more prone to acne. Washing the area with a Phisoderm cleanser can also help.

*See – Pimples, Stainless Steel Bowls,
Staph Infection and Zits*

Adoption - I love this topic. There are so many pets available, so please consider this option. Dogs come in many different ages, colors, and sizes. Some are already trained; others need more guidance. I suggest you treat an adopted dog like a new puppy for one week or more. Use the same door for potty training, block off rooms, and kennel the dog when you are away. Always remember when you bring an older dog (one year or more) into the home, don't just let it loose to run the house because the first thing it will do is have an accident. Watch it like a hawk until it is familiar with the surroundings. If there are other dogs living with you, be sure to introduce the tail waggin' roommates outside first and allow the resident dog its space. It may take two to three weeks for adjustment, and then the bonding process should occur.

Keep the dogs separated while you are at work or plan to be away because they may experience possessive, territorial feelings. In time they will be able to stay together safely in a relaxed atmosphere.

One more comment: don't cast away the idea of adopting an older dog because of its age. If you have the dog for one day, one month, or one year, you have given it the gift of life for that much longer. I, for one, love older dogs because they are settled and calm. A reputable agency always wants a win-win situation for you and the adoptee, so take your time picking a good match for you and your family. Choosing the right size, energy level, and personality is very important.

Aging - As your dog ages, you will notice it faces many of the same ailments aging humans face: arthritis, cataracts, incontinence, senility, and bowel issues. Please be watchful when letting an elderly dog outside due to its loss of sight and hearing. Tendencies to wander off into traffic, fall into swimming pools, or simply lose their way become commonplace in older dogs. Please make sure to have an identification tag attached to the collar. Weight control is vital to enable dogs to pick themselves up and be mobile. Potty accidents can become more frequent with older dogs, so extra trips outside are necessary. Returning to kenneling or confining your dog to a cleanable area when you are not home will make life easier. If your home has wood floors, you may notice its legs slipping out from underneath it. This is due to the pads of its feet becoming smooth and dry, making it hard for the dog to grip the floor. For larger dogs, this can be a big problem. A good idea is the use of carpet runners for your dog to walk on. This may not be "stylish," but it's temporary and beats putting your back out helping the dog up. A pad wax also is available at your local pet store to help moisten the pad and give grip to worn, dry feet, but follow the instructions closely. Often times with older dogs, you'll find yourself reverting back to the care you gave when they were puppies.

Aggressive Behavior - I have seen this behavior in puppies and also have watched it develop as a dog becomes confident at the age of two years. All I can tell you is it should not be tolerated. Aggressive behavior is very dangerous and can magnify if not corrected immediately. In a situation where multiple dogs reside together, one dog may become dominant, so remember: You are the alpha and you rule the kingdom. Never allow your confident pet, especially if you have multiple dogs, control the food, toys, and interactions in your home. Make getting on furniture and beds off limits. Correct aggressive actions as they appear, and don't hesitate to seek professional help if needed. The sooner any bad habit is dealt with, the less chance of reoccurrence. Remember, never tease the dog. Your role is to be the leader. Also, keeping the dog's collar and leash on will help control situations swiftly and put you in the dominant position.

They instinctively know the leash and collar mean business, which creates positive results when training. Aggressive behavior is a huge safety risk, not to mention a burden, when you have to constantly monitor the dog if unfamiliar animals or people are present in its domain. Keep it kenneled when visitors are at the home, especially children. This will ease not only you, but also your dog, as it can relax knowing it doesn't have to be on guard. Insurance companies are becoming very rigid about owning aggressive breeds, so I encourage you to be on top of this behavior. There is an excellent product on the market called the Gentle Leader that I have seen calm most dogs down instantly. It can be purchased at any pet store and is well worth its price. You the pet owner are ultimately responsible for the behavior of your pet and the law will not fiddle when it involves unruly, out-of-control dogs, so please make the effort to control and hopefully end this conduct.

Allergies - This is quite the buzz word. Many, many dogs suffer from allergies stemming from food to fleas to seasonal hay fever. Symptoms include sneezing and itching all over the place and biting and digging themselves so intensely that hot spots occur. There are allergy tests and shots available through your veterinarian; however, after a while these seem inadequate too. I believe a huge component is genetics, meaning whether your dog's parents suffer from allergies also. Recently, the grains in their food have been found to be disturbing as well. The itching and scratching can get so out of control that everyone is going crazy. I'm going to describe with some detail a couple different kinds of allergic reactions I often encounter. The first is yeast infections, which show up all year and commonly in more moist areas of the body. You probably find this in the ears, armpits, around the eyes, the vaginal area, the belly, and in many cases between the toes. The skin appears inflamed and red, and at time can have a blackish colored pigment. It also can be hot and smelly. The smoothness of the skin almost takes on a leathery, rough appearance. In addressing a yeast issue, I have some suggestions:

> 1. Change to a grain-free food. Your local pet

store can help you choose one. This means treats too.

2. Start your dog on a product called "Nzymes." They have a web page with more information. *See Yeast Infection.*

3. Shampoo with antifungal products, which can be found at pet stores or through online pet catalogs. Three of my favorites are: Zymox, Malaseb, and Vet Solutions.

4. Treat the affected areas with a topical antifungal cream purchased at any drug store, such as Lotrimin, Lamisil, or Monistat cream (used for women). After applying it, hold your dog for five minutes or so to allow the cream to penetrate and soothe the area. Use a cone if need be to keep the pooch from licking.

5. Purchase an ear ointment from petmeds.com or Lambriar Animal Health Care (also on the internet) called Zymox Otic. This stuff is fabulous and is one of the only meds available to you without a prescription. They will also carry the medicated shampoos.

6. Hang in there because I have witnessed remarkable changes in no time when you utilize these recommendations.

Seasonal itching usually occurs in the spring when the grass starts to grow and buds are popping out. This continues until the cold weather has set in for several days. During this time, fleas can be prevalent and contribute immensely to the itching and digging, even causing secondary skin infections to arise. My helpful hits for seasonal allergies are:

1. Always use flea treatment such as Frontline, Advantage, or Revolution faithfully.
2. Ask your veterinarian about using an antihistamine like Benadryl or one he/she would recommend.
3. Give a derm cap oil pill for the skin. Most pet stores sell them according the weight of your dog. I suggest using one bottle (at least sixty pills) to see if you notice any improvements.
4. Shampoo with an anti-itch shampoo, oatmeal soap or one recommended by your vet.

There may be times you have to see your veterinarian to get some relief for your pet. Just be aware that the pills or shot given to help calm the allergies could create a strong thirst leading to going potty more frequently. Keep your dog in a cleanable area in your home while away. I wish I could snap my fingers and give you the secret to make allergies disappear, but the best I can do is suggest you learn how to treat the symptoms in the early stages because they will reoccur yearly.

See – Blackened Skin, Cones, Fleas, Hot Spots, Yeast infections

Anal Glands - This topic really stinks. Remember watching your dog scoot his behind on your newly shampooed carpet and leave behind a brown streak? Or when you picked up your dog and all of a sudden there was a rank smell on your good shirt? Well, that is the "good" stuff from the anal gland factory. Every dog and cat has them and they are found on each side of the rectum, under the skin. These glands fill with a watery substance, and when they become full, they can leak or squirt out, alerting you by the odor. When you see the dog drag its "dupa" or smell this "wonderful" aroma, that means the anal glands are full and need expressing. Large dogs seem to be able to self-express more easily than small dogs. Nonetheless, your veterinarian or your groomer or even you can clean the anal glands, and I will tell you how. Cleaning the anal glands should be done in the bathtub so you can easily wash the behind.

> Step 1: Put the dog in the tub
>
> Step 2: Put a clothespin on your nose
>
> Step 3: Respectfully pull the dog's tail up to expose the rectum
>
> Step 4: With one hand holding the tail, take your other hand, cup it in front of the rectum, putting
>
> your thumb and middle finger on each side of the rectum. Push in with your fingers and pull outward. You may need to do this a few times to be sure it's all expressed.
>
> WARNING!! THE ANAL GLANDS HAVE BEEN KNOWN TO RELEASE UPWARD TOWARD YOUR FACE, SO BE READY FOR AN EYEFUL OF THIS WONDERFUL INGREDIENT.
>
> Step 5: Wash the dupa after cleaning the glands.
>
> Step 6: Your dog will give you the "fish eye."

Now there, you did it! I am proud of you.

A problem that may arise in some dogs is an abscessed anal gland. There are two kinds of substances in the anal glands. One is watery and the other is thick like paste. The dogs with the watery substance rarely have any problems with abscesses. But those with the thicker substance may. This occurs because the matter in the gland cannot be expelled. Your dog will let you know through its behavior by licking or biting that area or constantly sitting due to the pain. The best way to check for this is to lift the tail and look at either side of the rectum for a boil-like inflammation. It will be red, protruding like a pimple. See your vet because this will need to be flushed and treated with antibiotics. You will be surprised at how quickly it will heal, and your dog will feel so much better.

Anxiety - Oh yes, dogs have it too and in many forms. Some signs of anxiety can be: shaking, drooling, pacing, hiding, growling, snapping, running away, excessive whining and wetting. Many situations can cause anxiety, but the key word is FEAR. Storms, fireworks, shotguns, or any loud noises many times are the cause of severe anxiety attacks. I am not an expert on this subject, but I can't stress enough that you should get professional help as soon as you notice the anxiety. Cesar Millan and many qualified behaviorists are available via internet, cable TV, or DVD so you can see what to do and witness the results. You, the dog owner, have the ability with this knowledge to help your pet enjoy a relaxed life, which benefits the dog and you. The advice and training techniques these professionals offer really work. However, you must take the time to apply them. Anxiety is one of the leading reasons dogs are given up for adoption. And the sad explanation why anxiety develops and magnifies to such a horrible degree is usually the original owner's habits. For they did not take control of the issue right from the beginning and allowed it to become intolerable to live with. Now the anxiety is ingrained and the dog does the same thing to the next owner. And so it goes, on and on.

Fears and anxiety can happen at a very young age or many times not show up until mid life. Be aware during storm season and the holidays where fireworks and gun shots are part of the celebration. Talk to your vet about a tranquilizer if your pet is frightened and frantic. Also, placing the dog in its kennel can give it a safe place to relax and calm down.

Separation anxiety usually shows its ugly face in a young dog quickly. In fact, the shaking and drooling starts immediately when the pup is kenneled. And this is also when the behavior training should begin. But instead, most people feel sorry for the pup and remove it from the safest place it could be (the kennel); hence the anxious behavior increases. This fear is a lifelong problem if not corrected properly and immediately. Please take separation anxiety very seriously. Be alert to your puppy's behavior when you place it in its kennel. Drooling, digging, and biting at the kennel should never be allowed. Correction in the form of a firm command word should be used to help it learn calmness when in the kennel. Playing a radio and covering the kennel with a sheet will assist it in quieting down. This is a vital training procedure, and you must monitor the behavior each and every time to insure balance and harmony in your dog. Never remove the dog unless the conditions are calm. Practice placing it in the kennel several times a day, using the same procedure as if you were teaching it a trick. Reward it with praise each and every time you release it. Please be sensitive to the fears and anxiety of your dog. Seek help either from a professional or talk to your veterinarian for advice on how to eliminate this behavior. In the end, the main component is you and your willingness to succeed.

See - Bee Stings, Cage Anxiety,
Kenneling, and Thunder

Arthritis - This is a common problem amongst all sizes of dogs. It normally occurs with old age or an injury. Keeping your dog's weight under control is vital for ease of mobility. When our friends have stiff joints, I love the use of a joint compound containing Hyaluronic acid, which can be purchased at any pet store. This is administered according to weight. A noticeable difference should be obvious within a week to ten days. If not, change brands and find one that works for your pet. If old "Arthur" really is bothering the old bones, see your veterinarian for medication.

I highly recommend the use of a solid cooper choke collar around the dog's neck to aid arthritic dogs.

See - Copper Collars, Glucosamine,
Hyaluronic Acid, and Joints

Aspirin - This is a wonderful pill used mostly for pain and is also great for arthritis. Always use coated aspirin or baby aspirin for dogs. Talk to your vet to find out the dosage that is right for your dog's size.

*"Balance" - balance your life so you have
time to spend with your dog. It thrives on your
love and attention for its happiness.*

Baby Wipes - Buy them by the bunches. You can use them on you, your children, and your dog. Wipe your dog's face, butt, eyes, ears, or whatever is needed, then throw them away. They are a must.

Bad Breath - We all know about this one. Good, old-fashioned dog breath usually starts around five years of age and up. However, toy breeds can have it sooner. Puppies get a strong breath around five and a half months old because they are loosing their baby teeth. After a month or so you will notice it has vanished and the new pearly white adult teeth have arrived. Most of the time, bad breath is caused by dirty teeth; however diet and goodies can be a contributor.

Keeping your dog's teeth clean is vital not only for sweet breath but all around health. If you are able and willing, I highly encourage getting in the habit of either brushing or wiping your dog's teeth with a wash cloth dipped in diluted Listerine. This can help control the bacteria, which causes the odor. Recently a vaccination that helps control the odor-causing bacteria has become available from your vet, and I have witnessed great results.

Finally the easiest of all wonder cures that has caught my attention and works for dogs and cats can be purchased online through a company called Oxy Fresh. The product I'm talking about goes in the drinking water and treats the mouth with each drink. Impressive effectiveness is all I can say. You may order this at www.oxyfresh.com and the price is really reasonable. They also have a great toothpaste for us while you're shopping. Nothing like promoting sweet-smelling breath.

See - Teeth

Back - Back problems are very common among dogs, especially middle-aged to older ones. Almost every dog may have back issues at some point in its life. Longer bodied breeds are at higher risk than those that are short and thin. One of the main causes for back injuries is also one of the biggest problems in America today. You guessed it: weight. Do not over-feed your dog. Here are some signs of back issues.

    1. The dog is quiet and doesn't want to move much, but will still eat.
    2. The tail is down.
    3. The back is roached and tense.

They can hurt their backs in many different ways, such as climbing steps, jumping up and down on furniture, or chasing something. If you see signs of a painful back, keep the dog quiet and give it one baby aspirin for a small dog or one adult coated aspirin for a medium to large dog in the a.m. and the p.m.

Cut its food back by one-half because it will be getting absolutely no exercise for approximately three to seven days. Most of the time, this problem will get better on its own; however, this kind of injury is likely to reoccur throughout the life of the dog, so you might as well learn how to handle it.

With back and neck traumas, having to bend down to eat and drink can be very painful. Try supplying a raised bowl system, one at your dog's individual level. You will be thrilled at the degree of ease it offers. These bowls can be purchased at any pet store, or get creative and make one yourself. Also, the fierce and excessive shaking of toys or ropes will affect a dog's neck. Sorry to spoil the fun.

Backward Sneeze - This is a post-nasal drip which causes a spasm in the back of the throat. Your dog stops in its tracks and starts a sniffling, snorting sound while standing in a bow-legged posture. This episode can last as long as five minutes. Don't freak out: your dog is not dying when this occurs. Usually, the hay fever season is the triggering event. Here's a hint that usually works when your dog starts this snorting. Get peanut butter or soft cheese, apply it to the tongue and it should stop the spasm. Your vet can issue an antihistamine that can help.

Baking Soda - If itching is the main exercise, this works great in giving relief. Pour a generous handful of baking soda into a pail of warm water. Wash the dog with an oatmeal shampoo or soap-free shampoo. Rinse it thoroughly until the shampoo is gone. Then pour the soda mixture on the dog and towel dry.

Bandages - *See First Aid Kit*

Barking – Let's talk about this barking issue. How many of you have laid in your bed at night listening to the neighbor's dog bark for hours, wondering why doesn't its owner stop it from barking. It creates anger and annoyance when you should be in the relaxed mode. Please don't blame the dog for the behavior. All dogs bark; it's their way of communicating to show excitement or warn you of noises/visitors. However, some breeds tend to be very vocal, and if not taught properly, could become a real nuisance.

Every dog can be taught not to bark by diligent training or one of several brands of bark collars. I own a barker and decided the bark collar was my choice of controlling the behavior. Pet supply catalogs have a selection of bark collars to choose from, and they are fairly inexpensive. The brand I use is "Innotek" and it was only $45.99 for peace and quiet. If you use the bark collar, please realize this should not be a permanent collar. The dogs need relief from the prongs too. After a while of using the bark collar, the weight of the collar will remind the dog not to bark, so you then can loosen it. When using the bark collar for the first time, it is likely that your dog, when it barks, will squeal from the reminder the collar gives. Hold tight to your resolve, it will only take a few times before your dog understands the terms of the collar.

A good habit is to not allow your dog to be an obsessive barker from the get go. Barking incessantly is a sign of discourtesy toward your neighbors and guests and should be handled with immediate discipline. It's not easy to train your dog not to bark, and it requires you to be on noise patrol. Get yourself up from your chair while watching television and remove the dog from the area or put on the bark collar.

Dogs kept in outdoor pens tend to bark a lot. Pay attention: they're telling you they need a change in their surroundings. Take it for a good run, play ball, or do another activity. Your four-legged friend is begging you to give it a change of scenery. Remember that dogs need people to touch, love, exercise, feed, and water them. If you don't do this, you're shortchanging your pet and reneging on the dog owner commitment.

See - Exercise

Bathe - This is always one of the first questions asked when owning a dog. There are many different opinions on the issue. I personally tell pet owners that dogs can be bathed weekly, bi-weekly, monthly, or whenever you can't stand the dog's smell any more. I have been bathing dogs weekly for years without a problem of dry skin or loss of body oil. Many specialty shampoos used to treat skin eczema require bathing twice a week. So bathe away!

See – Grooming and Shampoo

Bee Stings - These nasty insects pack a punch, and they can swarm if the dog goes near the nest. Most stings are experienced in the same fashion as when humans get stung. The dog may hold its leg or paw out for a while, and swelling can even occur. Normally, by the following day all is well. Benadryl is the pill of choice for this problem. Talk to your veterinarian about the amount to use should this occur. However, if the dog has been attacked by a swarm and experiences multiple stings, head directly to the veterinarian immediately. Animals, like people, may go into shock after a sting, so keep a watchful eye.

Behavior Problems - Get out there and read up before taking on a dog. Most problems form because of lack of discipline, as well as lack of follow-through. Everyone usually takes the easy route. After one month or so, we tend not to pay as much attention to the dog because we are used to having it around and life gets crazy. Taking the time to ensure the dog uses the outside bathroom and watching that this actually happens can go to the wayside along with other things occurring in our mornings. Remember, you will be living with this friend for many years, so become committed with it in your home and get the help needed along with enjoying your dog. The first year is the hardest; you are forming the mold so do it right.

Be sure to take the time to tire this creature out. We all get up in the morning and get ready to start our day and rarely take the time to exercise them adequately after a night's sleep. Then off to work we go, eight hours later, we're tired and they have been kenneled all day. They're just busting at the seams with pent-up energy. Then, we wonder why the door, the shoe, or the magazine got chewed. Most behavioral issues wouldn't take place if we would just tire the dickens out of them. Please give this some serious thought. There are many behavioral experts who are willing to come to your home and give you instruction, but you have to follow through in order to manifest the results.

Belching - Yes, dogs belch too. It probably feels as good to them as it does to us.

Bile - *See Stomach Acid*

Birds (Large) - Hawks, owls, and eagles are licking their chops when they see those little creatures (kittens, puppies, or small dogs) running around in the yard. Always monitor small pets if you live in an area with these fine feathered friends. They have absolutely no problem swooping down and carrying off your little FiFi for supper. Prey is prey, and large birds don't distinguish between wild and domestic.

Biting - This is a really bad trait in a dog, but some do it. If you choose to live with the biting, you are responsible for the consequences. Keep your dog away from helpless children and smaller pets. Put the dog in a kennel when guests come over to the home. There are countless wonderful, kind dogs to love in the world, and a dog with a biting habit is very dominant or insecure, not a trustworthy companion. Please do not misunderstand what I am saying. Snipping is different from biting with a purpose in mind. Always seek professional help when evaluating your dog's needs.

If, on the other hand, your dog gets bitten and a puncture mark is left, clean it by cutting all the hair around the area, place peroxide on the puncture mark inside the bite (if possible), fill the puncture with triple antibiotic ointment until it pours out, and immediately see your veterinarian. Bacteria can become trapped inside the puncture wound, and it may not seem like a major injury, but infection can begin growing underneath the skin, causing an abscess.

See - Abscess

Black Hair - Just a reminder that the color black is a heat magnet, so always provide a shaded environment and be very selective about the temperatures in your vehicle when taking your dog with you. Heat stroke is lighting quick and can dehydrate or even terminate a dog's life in a frighteningly short amount of time. Wetting your dog down with cool water or keeping the hair short really helps. Also, I have found that dogs with black hair have more dander, so good baths and a derm cap (oil pill for the skin) work wonders.

Blackened Skin – Blackened, smelly, itchy skin indicates yeast.

See - Yeast Infections

Bladder Stones - If your dog has had bladder infection after bladder infection followed by surgery to remove bladder stones, diet control is the only remedy. It is important to have the dog's urine checked for Ph level by your veterinarian. Stick with a diet plan prescribed by your veterinarian and do not allow your dog to have table scraps, dog treats, etc. Also, use distilled water for drinking and pay attention to the flow or stream of urine exiting your dog. When you cheat and feed your dog whatever you want, sure as the sun rises, you can count on this reoccurring. Returning symptoms of bladder stones or infections will be nervousness, accidents, possibly with blood, frequent squatting around the yard, a trickle of urine coming out. Once you and the dog have experienced bladder surgery, train yourself to be aware of the urinary habits of your pet, for they are future warning signals. There are wonderful dog foods on the market to help control bladder issues. There are even recipes to make food if your dog does not like the prescription foods. My findings are that the prescribed foods produce long-term results.

See - Diet, Distilled Water, Urine and Urinary Tract Infections

Bleeding Nails- Having a nail bleed can be messy business. Nail trimming can create this easily. I've done it many times without intending to. The quick or vein that runs down the nail can be so close to the end of the nail, it is easy to cut. Dogs can break off a nail, which causes a real flood. Don't worry, it will eventually stop, but I suggest always having some blood stop in the First Aid Kit. It can be purchased at any pet store. Just gob it on the bleeding toenail and hold pressure for a moment to make sure it works. Keeping the dog quiet for a while, as in kenneling for an hour or so, will provide the time needed for it to cauterize. Peroxide or ammonia will remove any blood stain on fabric. You're welcome!

Bloating - If your dog seems very bloated, has a hard abdomen, and is acting extremely uneasy and panting, go to the veterinarian immediately. This could be a life-threatening problem, especially in large breeds. But if you find an empty dog food bag in the vicinity, get ready with the poop pail. Keeping the dog food where the dog cannot get to it is going to be your mission next time around. In the meantime, make sure the dog has a lot of water and go light on feeding for the next couple of meals. My crystal ball says loose stool probably is in your future. Get the poop pail ready and read up about the shop vac.

Bloating also can occur if your dog eats dead things outdoors. Vomiting and other fun bodily excretions will follow. Your veterinarian should have medication for this too.

Bloody Stool - Every once in a while our pets can have an intestinal flair-up very similar to what we experience. Feeding them different foods or table scraps or sometimes a virus are a few causes. You may notice blood in the stool and your dog may be straining to go potty. This is generally not life-threatening but does require some attention on your part. I would suggest offering some plain or vanilla organic yogurt along with a dose of Imodium or Pepto Bismol. Small dogs can have 1/4 cup of the yogurt; medium to large dogs 1/2 to 1 cup a couple times a day. Call your vet on the dosage of the Imodium per your size of dog. Then always start the healing diet of boiled ground beef or turkey mixed with rice to see if this corrects the problem. You should see your veterinarian if there is a reoccurrence or if the bloody stool continues for more than one day. Checking for parasites is in order too.

See - Diarrhea, Diet, Giardia,
and Soft Stool

Boarding - Let's face it: sometimes you need a vacation away from everything, so someone has to take care of your dog. I know some of you will not do this, but for those of you who do or will, here are some helpful tips. It is okay to leave your dog home, as long as you have arranged for someone to come into the home three to four times per day. Pay a neighbor, and don't be cheap. Have the dog-sitter come over before you leave so that you can go over instructions. Leave a radio on as well as some lights so the home seems normal to your pet. This should not exceed seven to ten days.

The next option is allowing a friend to take care of your dog. If this is your plan, take the dog over to the friend's house two to three times prior to leaving so the surroundings are somewhat familiar. If the dog is a runner, meaning it takes off like a bat out of hell, leave a leash on it at all times. Remember, your dog can be confused, and if the house has a lot of traffic with children running in and out, an escape right out the door could take place. Take time to get a temporary identification tag for the address where your dog will be staying, since no one will be home at your house to answer a phone call should your dog get loose.

Another option is boarding your dog at a facility. Let your pet visit the facility once or twice prior to your vacation date, if it's the first time leaving it, to help familiarize the dog with the smells and sounds of its temporary hotel. You will know when you pick up your dog if it enjoyed itself or not. I would suggest selecting a boarding facility with a 24-7 staff on the premises, along with an adequate area to go potty, and I mean *outside*, unless your dog is paper trained. Potty breaks are vital in my book to prevent a urinary infection that can occur from being nervous in unfamiliar surroundings. Boarding has gone to many new levels with video cams to view your precious one while on vacation. Feel good about where your pet is staying and go have fun on your vacation.

See - Identification Tags, and Urinary Tract Infections

Body Language - You know what I mean? Humans do it and so does every other animal on this planet. But the type of body language I am talking about is your dominant body language, being in charge of your dog. If you show fear, your dog feels it. If you act submissive, your dog becomes the master of the home, the walks in the park, the food, or anything within its surroundings. Be confident, take charge, and you and your pet will be happier. Dogs want a leader, so you need to play the part. Ease its mind by taking control.

Bones - I am not talking about the skeletal set-up of the dog here; I mean chicken, turkey, steak, and pork bones. These are all an absolute NO. The only ones I will endorse are the huge leg bones or boiled knuckles. However, if your dog should get into the trash (as mine have) and eat an entire turkey carcass on Thanksgiving Day, I can share some advice. My wonderful veterinarian taught me this trick, so I cannot take the credit. You need to feed the dog a huge portion of bread, cooked rice, and dog food. Note that the dog food should not be dry but soaked in hot water to make it like a sponge. All of this food will pack around the eaten bones and save your dog's life. Please believe me, as I have had to do this on three separate occasions. These bones are very sharp and could cause a lot of damage to your dog, so take heed. For the next few days, pay close attention to the behavior and bowel movements of this little piggy. Should the dog start to act out of sorts, see your vet.

Boric Acid (in powder form) - What a miracle chemical this is. It's safe to use with all your pets in killing and controlling infestations of fleas and a whole array of other insects in and around your home. Boric Acid can be found in farm and garden stores all over the U.S. I suggest always having it on hand in your cupboard. It comes in shaker containers for

ready use outside or inside your living area. There is
wonderful information online to fill your inquisitive mind.
See - Fleas

Buggy Eyes - Many dogs have buggy eyes. In my personal
experience, these types of dogs tend to have more eye
injuries due to the large exposed eye surface. These big,
beautiful buggy eyes have a tendency to pop out easily too.
Keep the eyes clean, as they catch more dust particles and
get more sleepers in the corners. Baby wipes and a few
drops of artificial tears (yes, the human stuff) are good for
cleaning out the eyes.

Burdocks - You know what these are even if you don't
recognize this word. Some are also called stick tights. The
dry remains of weeds that somehow have a purpose, I can't
even imagine what it is, and in the late summer all the way
into winter tangle themselves all through you dog's hair
creating a very picky and uncomfortable mess. My best
advice is to keep your dog's hair cut very short through the
burr season, especially hunting dogs with long feathers,
unless you like spending hours getting them out. It is
important that you do remove them, because if you don't your
dog will try very hard to bite them out and sometimes ingest
some of these picky devils. I don't suggest using scissors
unless you're very careful. Many a dog has accidentally had
their body lacerated from cutting too close to the skin.
However, you could slide the scissor blade through the clump
of hair several times to make combing out the burr easier.
Brushing and combing along with breaking apart the mass of
burs will eventually do the trick. But if it were me, I'd buy

my hound a haircut.

Butt Draggin' - Oh yes, we all are familiar with this one. The reason for this gracious dance could be one of three possibilities:

    1. The anal glands are full.
    2. Stool is caught on the hair surrounding the rectum.
    3. Yeast fungus is on the rectum skin.

      Always try to have the anal glands cleaned first, which alone will tell you if there's a stool issue. It is a must to clean the stool off the rectum area. If you are not able to do this, take your dog to a groomer or to a veterinarian right away. Usually only long-haired dogs have this problem. The third possibility is rarely diagnosed properly, so I will go into further detail. If your dog is dragging its butt on the carpet, then on the deck or driveway cement and it will not stop, it usually is a yeast fungus. You have to look at the rectum skin and check if it is red or even bloody from the wild abuse it has taken. To conquer the yeast fungus, use Lotrimin or Lamisil (a human cream found in the athlete's foot area of any store) on the rectum skin two to three times per day. Hold your dog for five minutes after applying the cream to allow it to absorb properly. I have noticed that dogs with this problem also have yeast in their ears, toes and around the eyes.

      See – Anal Glands and Yeast Infections

C

"Courage" - the fearless ability many dogs possess when faced with danger or pain.

Cage Anxiety - Cage anxiety is when your puppy or newly adopted dog obsessively drools until it is sopping wet when you arrive home from work. Other symptoms include digging and biting the cage nonstop, which makes their toenails bloody or breaks off a tooth. Don't ignore this behavior or assume that the dog will grow out of it because it will get worse. A dog with cage anxiety needs your attention and time. This behavior is not hard to correct with consistent training. I must say that it disappoints me, because most pet owners refuse to acknowledge it as an anxiety until it has gone too far.

If you own a dog with cage anxiety, start the training over and bring the cage out to be with you in every room you go in. Why? Because you will place the dog in it for just a few minutes and make it stay with the door open the same as you would teach it to sit or stay or lie down. Think of it as a trick you are teaching it. Place it in the cage several times and make it stay for two, then five, then ten minutes, and so on. Call it out by command and have a wonderful treat ready. Most dogs with anxiety get all worked up because they don't want to be separated from you. But remember: you are the boss and your dog is just fine sitting in its cage during training, even when you're home. When the dog accepts being

in the cage with the door open, try shutting the door while you are in the same room and go back to two and five and so on minutes for training. During these times, do not let your dog dig or bite the cage. It must sit or lie quietly. As you gain calmness, move the cage out of your sight and do the same training. In doing this, your dog realizes it is separated from you, so again do not allow any misbehavior during the timed sessions. With consistent training, you will gain the results you desire, and your dog will rest peacefully.
See - Anxiety and Kenneling

Calluses - They may be ugly, but we all get them, even our dogs. The dog usually has them on its elbows. A soft bed helps immensely, and also applying A&D ointment or bag balm (found at your local drugstore) can really do some healing. If these don't work, talk to your vet about a product called Kera Solv Gel. I've watched this do wonders.

Cat Stuff - This subject pertains to cat food and cat dung in the litter boxes. In case you haven't noticed, most dogs love to eat both of these whenever possible. I would suggest keeping these yummy snacks in an area your dog cannot get to. If possible, feed the cat up on a table or shelf high enough so it is impossible to reach with dog lips. And cover or gate off the litter pan for the same reason. Cat food is very high in protein and is not developed for a dog's body. Cat litter is not good to digest, not to mention the smell of the leftover on a dog's teeth and breath. Also the strong smell of cat urine will attach to the ears and muzzle hair, making for a not-so-cuddly pet. Use your engineering skills to create a feeding station and potty area that is dog-proof, and you will be glad you did.

Cataracts - If you own a dog older than ten years, you might notice a white cast that covers the eye. This is a cataract. It is very slow-growing and "Fido" will adjust wonderfully as its sight diminishes over a period of five years. As sight loss becomes more prominent, try to keep from changing your furniture around. The dog will learn the area as long as items remain in the same place. When venturing outside, it is the owner's responsibility to keep the pet away from dangerous pitfalls such as pools and traffic, or to make sure the dog doesn't simply wander off. If your yard isn't fenced, I would suggest getting a harness and tie-out to protect it. Prepare your family for these necessary changes to safeguard your friend.

There is a surgical procedure to remove the cataracts should your pet get cataracts at a young age. Check with your veterinarian.

Cherry Eye - This normally occurs in Cocker Spaniels, Shitzu, or Lasso Apso but can happen on any dog. Cherry eye is a little red bulge in the corner of the eye by the nose that protrudes from the lower eyelid. I suggest surgery to remove it. If left unattended over time, it can cause a lot of redness and clear mucus from the irritation of rubbing the eye. This is not an emergency or life-threatening condition, so use your own judgment and doctor's advice about when to take action. Again, keep your dog's eyes very clean by using artificial tears to wash the eye.

Chewing – This is a topic about a dog chewing at its body. A behavior that is sure to drive you nuts. Chewing usually is caused by allergies, fleas, or a yeast infection on the body and feet. A dog can chew a hot spot as big as a half dollar in a matter of minutes. Always check the dog's body for the location it is chewing. If it has chewed a hot spot, put some cortisone cream on the reddened area. Watch carefully, use a cone, or place a t-shirt on the dog to prevent further chewing in that location. You always need to check for fleas too, as flea allergies are very common. One flea can create a lot of havoc. Do not let chewing go on for too long. Get some help from "you know who."

See – Allergies, Cones, Fleas, Hot Spot,
and Yeast Infections

Chocolate Holidays - Halloween and Easter are big chocolate "free for alls" when your kids leave the Halloween bag or Easter basket in the range of your pooch to scarf up as much as it can. Remember, chocolate is very dangerous for dogs and can be fatal in some cases. Make everyone in the house aware of this danger and keep those bags and baskets up high and out of reach of your pet. It will definitely be a big savings to your pocketbook, not to mention all the vomit and diarrhea you won't have to clean up. That should be the biggest motivator.

See - Shop Vac

Choking - Choking can occur when your dog is trying to swallow a piece of rawhide that may be too big. Watch the chews and take them away when the size becomes dangerous or a choking hazard. Some dogs have a fetish for socks, pantyhose, or underwear. Who knows why? It is your job to pick up everything. You will save yourself a huge veterinarian bill and get some exercise bending. If you find your dog choking, open its mouth wide and try to grab whatever is the obstacle. Otherwise, get to the veterinarian fast.

See - Rawhides

"Cling-ons" - These are the fun little hard balls of feces that occur when the hair around the rectum is not kept short. It's important that a clean path is maintained for stool to drop easily. Ask your groomer if he/she would not mind trimming the hair around the rectum in between haircuts to avoid any problems.

See - Soft Stool

Cocker Nose - What the heck is Cocker nose? Again, this is my terminology because I commonly see this on Cockers, hence the name "Cocker nose." I don't even want to know the technical name for this and I'm sure it occurs on other breeds too. Cocker nose happens generally when the dog is up in years. The skin on the nose will start to rise up and get crusty. It is very tender if you try to pick it off. There is a cream from your veterinarian called Kera Solv Gel to help heal it as long as you apply it. The use of a cone may be needed for about twenty minutes to let the gel do its job.

See - Cones

Collars - There is such a beautiful array of collars available to use in today's market. All different colors, shapes, styles, methods of use, etc. All dogs should wear a collar if for no other reason than identification. Dogs love their collars, and they even know the sound of their own jewelry. Get your new dog used to one immediately. Check your puppy as it grows to so you can adjust the size of the collar. This holds true for adult dogs too. They can gain weight or muscle mass and require a different sized collar. Collars should never be too tight or so loose that dogs can slip out of them.

Be proud of your dog and keep the collar clean, since one of your dog's grandest pleasures is to roll in stuff and grind debris into the fabric of it. Have a spare on hand in case one gets misplaced or lost.

Collars can be dangerous if not used properly. A few problems to watch for are:

1. When chaining your dog outside, use a harness instead of a collar to avoid it getting caught up on something and choking;

2. Remove the collar before kenneling if your pet is anxious for the same reason; and

3. If your dog loves jumping in an outdoor kennel made of chain link material, use a harness.

Swimming a lot in the summer and wearing a leather collar can produce a rank odor around the ears/neck. If you have determined that there is no ear infection causing the odor, look to the leather collar as the culprit. When the leather collar does not dry out, the neck and ears remain wet, causing this area to retain a very strong, sour odor. This is because bacteria have formed on the skin due to constant moisture. Use a nylon collar during the summer months, and the odor should dissipate, along with shampooing the stinky area with an antibacterial soap a couple times a week. Also, keep the hair on the ears cut short, especially with Springers and Cockers, which will allow the ears to dry out, really making a difference in the smell of the ears.

Cones - I do not mean ice cream cones. This subject is about plastic cones that go around your dog's neck after an injury or surgery. Also known as E-collars or Bite Not Collars, these stop any biting of the body and allow injuries to heal. Everyone with a pet or a spouse should own one. This first aid supply is the greatest idea since sliced bread. I have found three different kinds. The most popular kind looks like a lamp shade, fits over the dog's head, and attaches to the collar to prevent your dog from chewing. However, it can be a nuisance for the dog to get food or water, not to mention getting accustomed to the collar. Another type is an inflatable inner tube restraint that you place around the neck. This one seems more comfortable for long-term use. The last type of device is a wide four- to eight-inch collar that prevents the neck from bending. These recovery collars have and do assist in the healing process of many, many dogs as long as you leave them on. Your pet will get accustomed to any one of these in a short period of time. My guess is it will be used more than once during your pet's lifetime, so hang on to it.

Confining your dog(s) - Have you ever been over to someone's house that has overly happy, kind of obnoxious pets that they refuse to confine? Well, friends, let's talk about this. You folks who own these bouncing balls of fur may not realize how intense their presence can be for your visitors. Have you noticed, when you do get occasional visitors, they either stay in their car or just stop in for a brief minute? I can tell you from hearing all the stories that your friends truly love you, your company, and even your home. But what they haven't told you, and this may come as a shock to you, is most of them can't stand your dogs and would enjoy their time with you immensely if while they were at your house you would confine your dogs. Keeping your pet confined is not a terrible thing. Dogs should not be allowed to pester, in an unruly fashion, guests you have invited over. Not everyone is a dog lover, and even those who really appreciate well-mannered dogs enjoy a dog-free gathering.

Quieting and controlling your dog is courteous to those in your home. Your canines will come to know this routine when company stops in if you train them. I personally have confined my dogs when friends stop by for the sole reason that we can enjoy our visit. When company stops by to visit with you, you don't want to spend an enjoyable afternoon reprimanding or yelling at the dog. This topic is not in any way a derogatory remark towards dogs in anyone's home. It is, however, a complaint I've heard mentioned to me once too often. Give this suggestion some thought, and I'm willing to bet you'll start to have folks stop over so much you might start letting the dogs loose once in a while.

Constipation - Everyone can relate to this problem, and yes it occurs in your dog too. Fiber, fiber, and more fiber. My favorite remedy is canned pumpkin. A couple of tablespoons for large dogs, a couple of teaspoons for small dogs, in the a.m. and p.m., will usually do the trick. A half teaspoon of ground flax seed meal on the dog's food also works well, but they do not like the taste as much. Another option that I've seen people have good luck with is switching your dog's diet to canned food rather than dry food. Do this very slowly to allow your dog to get acclimated.

Copper Collars - Dogs that are arthritic or geriatric can struggle to move because of old joints. Try putting a solid copper chain collar in the form of a choke chain around its neck. It's a holistic remedy used by humans for many years. I've put many of these on pooches and had wonderful reviews from their owners. You can order this copper chain online, but be certain that it's 100% copper and not copper-plated. Just Google "cooper chains" in your internet search.
Use a slip ring on each end like a choke chain, and drop the one end down through the other. Now there, your dog is off and running.

See - Arthritis

Coughing - Canine coughing is not something you want to hear. It could be a sign of a variety of issues, such as allergies, kennel cough, trachea problems, or heart issues. It is a good idea to have your dog vaccinated for kennel cough at least once a year. Hearing some coughing in the morning or after a nap out of your old buddy could be a sign of a heart condition. Let your veterinarian do an exam just to be safe. He/She will give you appropriate medication if needed. Trachea irritation is very common in toy breeds and can be dangerous. Request the expertise from your vet because he/she has medication to relax the trachea, giving you and your dog relief.

Cuts - These four-legged friends are very prone to cuts, especially hunting dogs. So here's some advice on how to clean and treat them: cut the hair away from the wound, poor peroxide on the area, dab carefully with a paper towel, and apply Neosporin or any other antibiotic ointment to the cut, then cover it with a gauze pad wrapped with a sticky bandage if possible (found in First Aid Kit). Check it every day for healing and apply more ointment. A cone may be needed to keep the dog from licking the bandage. Make sure that the bandage is not wrapped too tight. You may need to see your veterinarian if you feel it is more than you can handle.

See - Cones

*"Dedication" - the devotion and commitment needed
to raise our four-legged friends.*

Dandruff/Dander - Dogs can have those white flakes falling off their shoulders too. Usually what helps is a derm cap (oil pill) given daily and a weekly bath in a medicated shampoo. You can also use any over-the-counter dandruff shampoo, leaving it on the body for ten minutes. Rinse thoroughly after application. The results should be apparent in thirty days.

See - Derm Cap

Deafness in Dogs – Deafness is as common in dogs as it is in humans. Some are deaf due to birth defects, illness, injury or age. Certain breeds, such as Dalmatians, seem to have a greater risk to hearing loss than most.

If you suspect your dog doesn't hear or is losing its hearing, please take extra precautions to safeguard it. Attaching a bell to the collar will aide you in hearing where your pet is located. Also, do not leave your pet unattended outside as it cannot hear cars and other potential dangers that may be a threat to its well-being. Train your dog to be visual during interactions with you. Your dog will watch your hand gestures for guidance. Using a cable tie-out or keeping it in a fenced yard allows you to release your pet without concerns. Dogs are very keen and will use its other senses to acclimate to their environment. Don't pity your pet, it will adjust. Do your research to gain all available knowledge to insure positive interactions with your dog. Books and on-line articles are at your fingertips. Your pet can live a very full and productive life regardless of the hearing loss. However, it does need your leadership.

Deck - Gate your deck to create a playpen area. If your pooch is little, you may have to put a lattice or fencing on the bottom so it can't get through the rungs. This beats having to watch your flowers get eaten. It is also wonderful during the muddy season. You can let your dog out to potty and bring it up on the deck to enjoy the outside and stay clean too. What a bonus! A final note: just like any other activity, keep an eye open to prevent any deck chewing. Young dogs become bored quickly, and those railings are great to chew.

Derm Cap - These are oil pills that help with itchy skin and dandruff conditions. There are many different varieties that you can purchase through a pet store or pet catalog. It is an excellent product to use when your pet has allergies. They are sold in various amounts according to the weight of your dog.

Dermatitis - *See Eczema*

Diarrhea - The runs are absolutely no fun whatsoever for you or the dog. This development ensures a date with your shop vac. Diarrhea most commonly develops when the dog has managed to get into food or trash, or when changing from dry food to wet food without a slow introduction. Any change in food should be introduced over the course of five days, adding more of the newer food each day to make it easy on the intestinal system. Feeding rich table scraps to a dog that rarely eats them is usually not a wise decision. And unless you like the outcome I wouldn't offer them.

Stress or nervousness is a big culprit in creating loose stools too. When a dog's system gets anxious, it takes a toll on the bowels.

Melting snow creates water pooling on the ground, and all types of bird, rabbit, and dog doodoo is left stagnant, brewing quite the tonic for your dog to walk in. Licking or drinking this water can make your pet very ill. Contaminated water not only causes diarrhea but also vomiting. I have seen this crop up during the heat of the summer months too with stagnant water pools. Do not be surprised to see blood in the stool when the bowel becomes irritated. Not to panic: your dog is not terminal, but I would suggest your vet's special magic to make it disappear. Small dogs are at a higher risk because vomiting and diarrhea will cause dehydration. Many anti-diarrheal products such as Pepto Bismol or Imodium are handy helpers to keep in the first aid kit for minor flair-ups. Find out the amount from the doctor before the occurrence and write it on the label. Start a bland diet such as boiled ground beef/turkey and rice along with and any medications to complete the healing for a few days, and all should turn out fine.

See - Giardia and Soft Stool

Diet - This word has two meanings: 1) reducing intake to lose weight; and 2) the intake of certain types of food.

Let us start with the reduction of food for weight loss. We, as Americans, have very little discipline when it comes to food, be it for ourselves or our pets. This is an enormous problem in society and has trickled down to the poor dog that looks at us with those sorry, big eyes. The sad story is many of us refuse to change until something terrible occurs. Your dog doesn't need a treat every time it goes potty or looks at you cross-eyed. Don't follow the food manufacturer's instruction for amounts to feed either. Watch your dog's body because every dog should have some curves to it. You'll feed large amounts when it is young and active, but by three years and up, you should start cutting back on the volume. Quit scraping dinner plates in the bowl too. Why not just put your dinner scraps in the compost pile?

There are many choices of dog food in today's market. If you have a healthy dog, you have many good brands to choose from; however, the better the brand, the less stools created. Many of the less expensive foods are packed with fillers, which in turn create more stools. So, if you don't like to scoop poop, buy the better brands. As dogs age, you most likely will have to change their diet again. New wonderful recipes for sensitive stomachs, weight loss, and senior diets, which contain less protein to aid with the aging kidneys, are all available in stores today. Find a staff member with nutritional knowledge to help you with your choice. Allergies can flair up intensely and the food can play a big role here. There are many varying viewpoints on what to feed when allergies are present. I've seen wonderful results when you use grain-free diets. The belief is that grains are not needed and not available in the wild, and possibly a leading factor for allergies in our pets. Talk to the experts at the feed store, and they can help you decide on a product to introduce.

Try one bag to see if your dog shows signs of relief, and don't forget to mix it in with the old food for a few days. You should see results in two weeks. I have to mention how thrilled I have been with the evidence my clients have had. Many ear issues where yeast was present have completely cleared up with the change in diet. There are prescription foods, sold through the veterinarian, developed to address specific health problems, i.e. kidney, liver, intestinal, or heart, etc. I urge you to follow the doctor's orders if your pet has been issued this type of food because it will not only improve, but extend your pet's quality of life.

Some of you feed your dog people food because you say it won't eat the dog food. The truth is you give in and start feeding it people food, and before you know it, your dog is turning its nose up to any dog food. If you love feeding your dog people food, here is a recipe that is healthy, and your dog will love it.

Recipe:
1 lb ground round or ground turkey
4 cups cooked brown rice
1 frozen bag of mixed vegetables
Boil the ground meat in a pan of water for 5 to 10 minutes. Add the frozen vegetables for an additional 5 minutes. Cook your brown rice. Drain the meat and vegetables, mixing with the rice. When the food cools, bag it up in freezer bags according to the amount you feed your dog and freeze it. You can take out enough for each day and cook the food weekly or bi-weekly.

A toy dog receives 1/4 to 1/3 cup total per day; a small dog needs a total of 1/3 to 2/3 cups per day; a medium dog needs 1 to 1 1/2 cups per day; and a large dog needs a total of 3 cups per day. I already see you rolling your eyes about the amounts, but if you follow the instructions, you will have a great looking, svelte dog. Plus this leaves more room for treats.

The Raw Diet also is up and coming. Feeding your pooch raw meats and no grains takes the dog back to the days of its origin. If any of these sound encouraging do some research and give one a try.

One important tip for you: always, always blend any new food in slowly with the former food over the course of five days to avoid any gastrointestinal upsets. If you do not heed this warning, *see Shop Vac.*

Digging - As in digging the hell out of your yard. Dogs dig for various reasons. Some that come to mind are: to escape under the fence, to get an animal, to cool their bodies in the heat, and lots of times because they are just plain bored. Leaving them unattended for too long is the first mistake most pet owners make. It's in dogs' nature to dig and discover or hide things. I've found monitoring your dog diligently for the first year can stop the behavior before it becomes a habit. It takes a lot of time and effort, but it works. Being attentive by going to the window and watching every five minutes or so and catching your dog in the act is how it is done. Have the gumption to go out and give the NO DIG commands, and if need be bring the dog inside for you to monitor. The whole idea is to stop even the thought of digging. Change the plan or give the dog something else to do. In other words, take the attention off digging with other fun ideas. If you do not do this, your yard will look like a mine field, and once again the fault ultimately will be yours.

Discolored Hair (Reddish) - When I see a dog with a reddish tint to its hair, especially around the mouth, eyes, feet, legs, and the hair around the rectum, I know right away it has been licking itself or chewing. The saliva turns the hair a reddish brown in the areas that are being licked. What to do about it? First check for fleas, because if your dog has an allergy to them just one flea will raise Cain on its body. When fleas are not present, then it is usually yeast on the skin, between the toes and around the rectum. A change of food to one with less grain will make an enormous difference. Treating the areas of skin with an antifungal cream once or twice a day is very helpful. Big water drinkers can have a lot of stains around the mouth if they have long hair. Keeping the hair shorter will improve this and also help with dripping. It will take some time, but if you get on the right track, the red will grow out and the hair will be its beautiful color once again.

See - Allergies, Diet, Eyes, Fleas, and Yeast Infections

Distilled Water - You can buy it in the store or boil water in a pan for a few minutes to make it yourself. Dogs with bladder conditions should drink distilled water. It really seems to help stop the occurrence of bladder or kidney stones, along with following a strict diet from your vet.

Doghouses - I am not a doghouse kind of gal, but I do realize there are dog owners who use doghouses. My hope is for all doghouses to be grand and proud places in appearance, containing insulated walls and plenty of ventilation during the summer. Please, please make sure to keep your dog warm in the winter and cool in the summer. Use straw for warmth, and pack the house full. Placing bales of straw around the outside of the whole house during the winter will not only block the wind, but the straw will keep the house toasty warm. Use of a tarp to block wind and sun is a wonderful idea too. It's inhumane to leave your dog with the sun beating down on it without any form of shade. Be creative in the making of your doghouse. You can put windows in it and run electricity to it for a radio or fan. Go ahead and call me obsessive or overboard, but your dog loves a fan blowing on it in the hot summer, just like we do.

Doggy Diapers - Just like aging people, many a dog becomes incontinent with age or due to a health issue. To help you through these wet times, purchase some wonderful diapers tailor-made to fit all sizes of dogs. They are very absorbent and will be extremely helpful when you can't be home to do potty patrol. You can find the diapers at any major pet chain.

See – Incontinence

Drool - If you like being slimed, pick a breed that drools a lot. Drooling can be caused by many factors: nervousness, smelling or sniffing a scent, drinking water. Be sure when selecting a dog that you know which ones drool more than others.

Dry Eye - It is just that, an eye that starts to lose the lubricant that allows it to pivot and move smoothly. My own personal assumption is Dry Eye occurs more commonly in dogs with allergies. Usually you will notice some extra rubbing of the eyes, and more accumulation of eye matter appears. I highly recommend seeing the veterinarian for drops to help control this. In the section about eyes I have listed some medications I have found work wonders.

See - Eyes

*"Energy" - the interaction of invisible forces
between you and your pet.*

Ears - These incredible little radars have the intense ability
to express so many feelings, and they come in all shapes and
sizes. Upright, flip flop, half-cocked, so long in length they
slap the ground, thick and heavy, and pointy with sharp
features. Twisting and turning, rotating to hone in every
possible vibrational pitch with the utmost accuracy and
clarity. They are also a breeding ground for all types of
bacterial "ick" and can become really smelly, red and itchy, or
clogged with a lot of black thick wax. If your dog fights ear
issues, it's important you learn how to treat them because it
can be a lifelong reactivating menace with one or both ears.
There is a good chance that a dog with ear infections also
has allergies. I recommend keeping the hair on the ears cut
very short, such as with Cockers and Springer Spaniels, to
allow more air to flow through. A dog that swims a lot can
have "swimmer's ear," so after a day of swimming is done, use
an ear drying product from any pet store. If your local pet
store doesn't have this product, you can mix one part alcohol
with one part white vinegar.

   Yeast infections in their ears can flair up throughout
the dog's life. This type of infection manifests quickly,
making the ear flap red and irritated and sometimes crusty
with an orange smelly wax. The dog will dig the heck out of

its ear or shake its head a lot, which is an indication to you to check the ear out. There is a wonderful ear ointment you can order from PetMeds.com, or Lambriar Vet Supply (Phone 1-800-344-6337) called Zymox Otic that is developed just for this type of yeast infection. I use it regularly and would recommend the blue bottle of Zymox because of the hydrocortisone that is added. Hydrocortisone relieves the terrible itching of the ear and the other goodies treat the infection. Also a change of food to a grain-free diet is a must if you are looking for long-term results, and this includes treats. I have seen ears clear right up with a food change. A good feed store will have this type of food.

Another type of unsightly ear development involves an unbelievable amount of dark wax deep in the ear canal. Both of these make the ear very tender, so close attention is needed. To clean the ear at home and remove all of the wax, you need to have an ear cleaner from your local pet store or your veterinarian. The ear cleaner that I have had great success with is called Foaming Ear Cleanser by Animal Dermatology Laboratories, and you can get this from your veterinarian. Hopefully, they have it in stock or can order it for you. It is fabulous. Start by generously applying this cleanser to the inside of the ear and massage it for a few minutes. When you turn the ear over, start cleaning the flap and inner ear with baby wipes. Repeat if a lot of wax is present. Apply any medication after cleaning. This cleaner totally degreases the hair on the ears after using an ointment also. Use the cleaner like a shampoo on the greasy ear and then rinse. I also have used baby oil with great success in cutting through the thick ear wax.

Most ear infections will need medical attention to

clear them up, and having some of the ointment on hand is helpful to catch it in early stages.

Ear mites are a common occurrence in many pet's ears. The mites look like small particles, similar to coffee grounds. There are ear mite products at any pet store. Use the product as directed.

After cleaning your pet's ears, always watch for ear flapping because it can cause a large hematoma on the ear flap. Flapping is when your dog shakes its head and the ears hit each other with such force that it causes fluid to build. The ear becomes fat and full of fluid. If you notice this behavior, place the lamp shade cone on your dog and call your vet for the amount of Benadryl to administer to calm down the head shaking. It is vital you stop the head shaking or a visit to the veterinarian will be in order.

See - Cones, Diet, Hematoma, and Yeast Infections

Eczema - This is an issue with many breeds and is related to allergies. Eczema normally attacks the thick-coated dogs, and age is not a helpful factor. If you have been told your dog has eczema, keep the hair short in the infected area and shampoo with medicated shampoo such as Tegrin or Selson Blue (yes, the people stuff). Or if you wish to use dog shampoo, try Sebolux, Relief, or Oxydex ordered from an animal catalog/website. Your vet may prefer one over the other. Shampoo your dog weekly, leaving the suds on the skin for five minutes, and pick away any scabs while working in the shampoo. If your pooch has a severe case of eczema that is in many areas of the body, consult your veterinarian. I have seen excellent results when antibiotics were prescribed.

Extreme chewing on its feet with red irritations between the toes is generally a sign of a fungus. To treat this aggravating symptom, use Lotrimin AF or Lamisil between the toes. Eczema or fungus can take on the appearance of ringworm, a raised red circular band on the skin. Treat this with the same ointment twice daily on the infected area. After applying the ointment, hold your pet for five minutes or so, allowing the meds to work their magic. I have done this treatment with wonderful results. A grain-free diet is very helpful for eczema.

See - Yeast Infections

Elastic Bandage - There is a great bandage sold in some pet stores, but I normally find it in horse supply stores. This bandage sticks to itself and stretches like an ace wrap. It is a must to have in the First Aid Kit and comes in a variety of bright colors. Be sure not to wrap it too tightly. This bandage works great for people too.

Electric Cords - TV, lamp, clock radio, or even extension cords are potential hazards for young dogs. They walk by them and just decide to pick them up in their mouth, chomping down with quite a buzz. Young dogs can be horribly injured from their playfulness. Please do a safety check when taking on a new puppy, for them and also for you. This is another reason why kenneling is so important when you are not able to watch them.

Electric Fences (or Invisible) - Whoever thought of this type of fence was a genius. You can keep your dog home, yet give it the freedom to run. Many neighborhoods allow only these types of fences due to building codes. There are three comments I can make.

1. Take the collar off if you take your pet in the car, because it will get zapped if you don't.

2. Your dog can get attacked by another dog coming into your electric barrier, (which we know can happen), so know your neighborhood dogs around you.

3. Larger dogs have been known to just run through the fence after something, and they won't cross back into their yards because of getting zapped. Please note that I am not being critical of this method.

I am mentioning incidences I have known to happen. You can hire the installation and training, or you can do it yourself. These fences also can be used inside of the house for room boundaries. I highly recommend these types of fences for the safety and control of your dog.

See – Deck and Fencing the Yard

Emotions - Do dogs have emotions? You bet your boots they do. Not as many as we have, but a lot of the same basic ones we experience. Happiness, fear, and anger are a few. Unlike humans, however, dogs don't behave in certain ways to punish us. For example, your dog may have an accident in the house when you leave, and you decide it did this to get back at you for leaving, as if the dog is thinking, "Okay, you're leaving me alone so I'll show you and poop on the floor." That's your human reasoning taking over. Your dog poops on the floor because it's anxious, and this is an expression of fear. There are a lot of great books available to you in the library or bookstore to assist you in understanding the dog's way of thinking and expressing its emotions, which is a really huge communication concept. I urge you to read up in this area and you'll find it a fascinating topic. You'll also understand your beloved pup better.

Energy - We live in an energy-based world. Your dog knows this more than you. It can tell dominant energy from submissive energy, happiness from fear, safety from danger. The emotional energy you give to your dog is going to determine many responses you get in return. Giving fear energy allows the dog to be dominant over you. However, in reverse, you'll see the dog become submissive. Pay attention to your energy with any animal; it's fun and an interesting way to communicate. Loving energy always prevails.

Epsom Salt - If you haven't heard of this fantastic product before now, get it because there is nothing better for our sore feet and body to soak in. It is the best drawing agent I have ever used. If your dog ever has any kind of cut or abscess, use Epsom Salt as a hot compress on a wash cloth a couple times a day. It really is a miracle.

Euthanasia - I can see your eyebrows lifting and that nasty smile on your face—you're thinking about your ex, aren't you? I would just like to mention a few suggestions to help ease this very emotional process. As the quality of life diminishes for your dog, most owners can't help but ponder thoughts about this issue, and I feel being somewhat prepared is helpful.

I recommend getting some tranquilizers for your dog from your veterinarian. The purpose for these pills is to make your pet very relaxed and sleepy so the anxiety is gone.

This also helps in easing your mind and emotions. Transporting your beloved pet to the veterinarian when it is tranquil will make that journey so much easier. Give the pills approximately two hours prior to your appointment so the tranquilizers have ample time to take effect. If your choice is to go to your clinic without a relaxing medication, consider asking for a sedative injection of some type when you arrive in the examination room. This can and should be a very peaceful experience for all of you. Many vets will come to your home for a fee, helping to ease in this emotional endeavor. You may choose to cremate your dog with the option for return of ashes or take it home to its resting place, whichever is best for you. There are wonderful caskets, urns, and markers available on the market. Pet stores and catalogs can help you with this very personal memorial. Pet cemeteries are also available in many towns.

Exercise - Imagine this: you have worked a long, hard day, running your children to and fro, and you finally reach home only to be greeted by your dog, which has been waiting and waiting for this moment. It may seem like this is just another job needing to be done for the day, but it is a vital part of dog ownership. Dogs need to have plenty of exercise or trouble will occur, such as chewing, barking, or wild behavior. Small dogs can run through the house and get a lot of energy burned off, but larger dogs need to run or go on a long walk. Younger dogs require an enormous amount of exercise to feel content. A dog that does not get the proper amount of exercise and owner time can become bored, anxious, or depressed and begin acting out. Take the time and make both of you happy. The behavior in the home will be much calmer with proper exercise. You'll start to notice after the energy has been released your pet will also focus much more intently on the commands you give.

Excessive Thirst – Your dog empties its bowls of water as soon as you fill them. You can't help but notice the craving your dog has for water. Potty accidents are taking place more often. In an older dog, this thirst could be a form of diabetes, kidney failure, or Cushing's disease (to name a few). Testing for Diabetes Insipidus should be on the list of possibilities to be considered as causes for the thirst. I mention this one because it is often overlooked or not even known by some animal clinics.

Puppies are not immune to having a health development either. Excessive drinking is not the normal behavior for young dogs. Definitely consult your veterinarian on this and ask for a simple blood screen. It will be to your advantage to know, especially if you have purchased an expensive pup. Most breeders will make it right with you by issuing a refund or another puppy. It is important to check this out and get your dog on the right food and/or medication to help control this matter and aid in your pet's quality of life.

Eyes - A lot of subject matter here so get a glass of wine and have a seat. How beautiful these eyes are, full of expression, love, and wisdom. Keeping them clean is important to the health of the eye. Hair should be kept away, along with sleepers, as they both cause irritation leading to bacteria in the eye. Take notice that the white of the eye should always be nice and white. Seeing redness occurring could be the sign of an agitation. Washing the eyes with artificial tears, found at the drug store, daily is excellent in helping cleanse dust and debris from the surface of the eye. An ointment found in the pet catalogs called Teramycin is wonderful to have and keep in your First Aid Kit; this is used for minor eye irritations. Dogs with big round buggy eyes gather more than their share of dust and pollen due to the large eye surface, so they're going to need more attention in keeping them clean.

Many breeds, such as Pekinese, Shitzu, and Bulldog types, have folds of skin on each side of their short noses. Eyes that are runny can create wetness in those folds, producing a strong, sour odor on the face. These folds can become very red and tender due to the constant wetness. Keeping this area clean and dry is impossible and on a white dog it is sure to be discolored. I have witnessed this disappear with the use of tetracycline issued by some veterinarians. Talk to your vet about it. The dog owners I have known were very happy with the results and mentioned their pets felt better too.

Dogs as well as people develop all kinds of eye complications. Two very frequent types are corneal ulcers and dry eye. Corneal ulcers are commonly caused by a poke or scratch to the eye. This is very painful to your pet and the inability to open the eye along with excessive tearing will occur. If you notice these symptoms, make an appointment a.s.a.p. Quick attention will benefit the healing of the eye and limit the discomfort your dog is feeling. Being faithful in dispensing the medication your vet has issued will be vital to the healing of this eye injury. Don't get discouraged. Some corneal scratches can take a while to clear up, and your furry friend may start to hide when the eye meds appear.

Outsmarting your dog to apply the eye medication might become a regular pastime. Leaving a leash attached to the dog's collar during the treatment will give you a way to get it out from under the bed with ease.

Dry eye is the next eye problem that can occur in any dog, although some breeds seem to be more apt to develop it than others. I have noticed a very high percentage in dogs with allergies. Generally this appears in elderly dogs seven years and older, but I have known it to occur in some three to five years of age. The eye will start to contain more matter on a daily basis, and sometimes a thick mucus substance will be present. Your dog will want to rub and drag the eye on the carpet or furniture to itch it, which can cause an eye injury. Unlike the ulcer, dry eye is not painful and usually the eye is held open. Special medications are required with dry eye to maintain lubrication. Two that I would recommend you try through your vet are Tacrolimus and Pilocarpine Ophthalmic Solution. The results for one or both of these are remarkable. Any over the counter drops for severe dry eye can be used until you can get in to the doctor. You will need to treat the dry eye condition two to three times a day for the rest of your pet's life. The good news is if you're faithful it can be controlled.

There are cases where genetic blindness can develop almost overnight, and you will notice the dog bumping into things it could see just a month earlier. This can be quite an adjustment for both you and your dog. Wonderful books have been written on this subject and even more great information is available online to help you acclimate your pet to its surroundings and use guided command words. You may witness anxious behaviors and distrust for a while, but most dogs settle in with time. This type of deficit can be a challenge to both you and your dear friend. Please practice patience and understanding during the re-training period. Your veterinarian is always there to help with any questions you should need answered. Cataracts and nearsightedness happen in many dogs too. Read the follow-up articles on these topics in this book.

See - Buggy Eyes, Cataracts, Cherry Eye, Dry Eye, and Nearsightedness

Farts
Fatty
Fatty Tumors
Feet Lickers
Fencing The Yard
Fireworks
First Aid Kit
Flash Lights
Fleas
Food
Foot
Frequent Thirst
Frequent Urination
Fungus

*"Faith" - the deep, unwavering belief that
all is well and training will pay off.*

Farts - I didn't do it, did you? Who did it? Go ahead—just
blame the dog.

See - Gas

Fatty - Here is what I am told when a dog is overweight: "My
dog is not fat, it's solid." The truth is that a majority of dog
owners overfeed their dogs for numerous reasons. I even
see extremely thin dog owners with obese dogs. Figure that
out. Okay people, listen up: ALL DOGS BEG and will continue
to do so. You are the boss of the domain, so just say NO.
Many a dog will eat and eat, so it is up to you to measure an
appropriate amount of food that will maintain a healthy
weight. A dog should only eat once or twice per day. As your
dog ages, like us, weight is easily accumulated. The solution
simply is to cut back on the food. Remember, the amounts
listed on the food bags do not pertain to all dogs. If you
have a puppy (six to twelve weeks), feed it at least twice per
day, increasing the amount of food according to its growth.
If your puppy tends to be "roly poly," you may always have to
watch its food intake, because even puppies can be overfed.
People are amazed that an older dog (ten years and up), i.e.,
the size of a Cocker Spaniel, can maintain its perfect weight
with as little as 1/3 cup of food twice daily.

This also varies with activity level. You have to reduce the amount of food until you see the drop in weight. For example, a full-grown Labrador in its elderly years may only need 1 1/2 cups per day to retain a healthy weight and mobility. The lighter your dog is, the easier it is on its joints and movement. I already see your eyes bugging out. Look for body contour and shape, and I guarantee your friend will live much longer.

See – Diet, Exercise, Joints, and Obesity

Fatty Tumors - These tumors are round in shape and usually movable under the dog's skin. They are nothing to cause any worry. Fatty tumors usually start appearing around seven years of age or older. They grow in stages and can become quite large. Some dogs produce a lot of them, others just a few. Keep up with yearly visits to your veterinarian to check the tumors as well as get advice on whether to remove them.

See - Lumps

Feet Lickers - Why do they do this? For two reasons: habit and possible irritant. Licking feet can be a calming cleaning action; however, many times I find a very red, irritated itchy yeast in between the toes. The first solution would be to change the food to a grain-free or vegetarian food. Also treat the fungus with cream from the store. Lotrimin or Lamisil applied twice a day to these areas can work wonders. Dogs with long hair between the toes need to have it removed so the creams can be applied to the red area. Use the cone for ten minutes when treating with the cream so it can start the healing, and to keep your dog from licking the cream right off. Summer months, when allergies are high, create the problem, and believe me, it's very bothersome for our pooches. If the foot licking gets severe, see your vet for help.

See - Yeast Infections

Fencing The Yard - A boundary or barrier made of wood, chain link, or these wonderful maintenance-free plastics not only enhances your home but will create a safe haven for your dog. You can erect them yourself or contract out. However you decide be sure that the fencing meets the ground to prevent escapes and that the gaps at corners or near the house are also tight. Judging the proper height for all the jumpers is vital too.   It's important that you figure in all the must-haves so the expense and effort of installing the fence is not in vain. I am a huge lobbyist for any type of fence to give your dog the feeling of freedom and you peace of mind. Remember to watch and train those happy pups that there will be no digging the yard or excessive barking while enjoying this wonderful play area. Keeping the poop pail handy is a must and should be done daily to prevent the tracking of this fertilizer into your home.

See – Deck, Electric Fence, and Runaways

Fireworks - I personally love them because they are a wonderful form of entertainment, but dogs usually hate them. A dog's fear of fireworks may not be a problem early on in life but may arise when it's middle aged. Running away along with damage to your home can happen totally out of fear. Be prepared by housing your pet in its kennel with a radio on to drown the noise. Consult with your vet about the

use of a tranquilizer during these high-stress times.
See – Anxiety and Thunder

First Aid Kit - You can call me neurotic, but I believe in always being prepared (I was a good Girl Scout). A First Aid Kit for your dog is a must in my book. You should travel with it, keeping one in your car and home. What should be in this Kit? Here is a list of items everyone should have:

> Artificial tears
> Aspirin (coated or baby)
> Baby wipes
> Bandages (elastic and standard)
> Benadryl
> Blood Stop
> Cotton balls
> Cough syrup
> Dramamine
> Flashlight (best if the head lamp variety)
> Imodium
> Lotrimin AF (for fungus)
> Medical tape
> Pepcid AC
> Pepto Bismol
> Peroxide
> Pliers
> Prescribed medications
> Q-tips
> Scissors
> Sterile gauze pads
> Syringe

Teramycin (for eyes)
Tranquilizers
Triple antibiotic ointment
Tweezers
Wire cutters (small)

If you are a hunter, you should carry the following additional items: powdered electrolytes (add to water), ear flush, pad wax, and if possible, antibiotics.

This may seem like a lot of things to have on hand but you will be glad when you need it. Alter your First Aid Kit as you see fit. I listed items that are handy.

Flashlights - This is a subject that usually is funny in the beginning but can turn into an obsessive behavior. Many dogs have a great time chasing the beam of light around when you have your flashlight on. And I will agree it is very funny. However, this can become an extreme obsession to the degree that you need professional help to gain your dog back. Be careful about the focus your dog has for this fun innocent game.

Fleas - Oh no, a FLEA!!! What a huge subject this is. I'm going to try to make this simple for those of you that don't know what a flea is. A flea is a very small brown insect that jumps and loves to take up house on many creatures, i.e., dogs, cats, squirrels, rabbits, etc. Our pets pick them up when they are outside moseying around on the lawn. These little pains in the "you know what" are worse in the southern states or warmer climates than in the cold states, and fleas can become a big problem in your home if you don't treat with preventatives and stay on top of it. They are very hardy and can live a year in your home without a host. If your dog has allergies, one bite from a flea can put it into an itching frenzy for days or weeks until you get medication from your vet. There are fantastic products on the market today to help control fleas that get onto your pet. These products should be used faithfully every thirty days, especially in high-risk areas. I also like to use a product called "Cap Star." This fabulous substance is a pill you give according to the weight of your pet, and it starts killing the fleas within thirty minutes. If you ever had a flea infestation in your home, you'll understand how vital it is to stay on top of these insects. Check your pet's body all over, especially on the belly area and head. Watch for fast little bugs scurrying on the skin and black pepper-like droppings, which are dried blood (the excretion from the flea). If you see the droppings, somewhere there is a flea. "Cap Star" is your friend here, and it can be ordered through many pet catalogs.

Now here's a trick you can learn for when you go flea hunting on your dog's body. Get one or two Q-tips and dab them with Vaseline; then when you spot a flea, just dab it with the Vaseline. Now you've stopped it in its tracks. These bugs jump, so you don't want them to jump onto your floor or carpet. The Vaseline smothers the fleas so you can pick them off without losing them. Flea hunting can be entertainment; it's in the same category as zit picking. Some of us like it and some of us don't.

If you should find a few fleas on the pooch, don't overreact and tent the house for fumigation; most likely that's all there was. But if you see some fleas every day and you have used liquid flea killer (Frontline or Advantage), get hoppin' on the "Cap Star" and treat your yard too, because as I mentioned before, this is where the dog picks up fleas— while lying in the grass. Here's how to check your house for fleas. Take a pie tin, put soapy water in it, and place it on the floor where the pet tends to spend time or sleep. Now get a desk lamp with a goose neck and turn it on with the light about three inches above the soapy water. The fleas will hop towards the light and fall in the water, allowing you to see how many you catch. You can move these traps all around the house or make a few of them. This can be a science project for the whole family. If there's a lot, you should call an exterminator for the best results. However, there are always your do it yourselfers and for this I would suggest one of two treatments. Most good pet or feed stores carry a home flea treatment and flea bombs to use. Follow the instructions and find out whether you need to leave the house for an amount of time. If you have a minor problem, many people use boric acid in powder form found in garden or farm stores. Again, follow all directions. I suggest checking from time to time with your homemade flea trap just for peace of mind. The most important information I can relay to you is, always check your pet's body for droppings and fleas. Be aware and stay on top of this, especially in high-risk seasons. Remember all warmer climate states have flea activity all year. Northern states generally through the summer and fall months or until cold weather sets in for the winter. I know you're scratching your hair right now so try to imagine how your dog feels with those little devils crawling on it.

See - Allergies and Boric Acid

Food - *See Diet*

Foot - *See Aging, Chewing, and Feet Lickers*

Frequent Thirst - *See Excessive Thirst*

Frequent Urination - The need to go potty a lot and while outside going in several different areas, along with some accidents in the house, usually is an indicator of a possible bladder infection. Pacing, anxious behavior, and whining are all warning signals that need your attention. When you know your pet is acting out of sorts, call your vet because a bladder infection could be the cause. These infections are painful and should be dealt with right away.

Other causes for frequent urination are Cushing's disease, diabetes, and kidney failure, just to mention a few. These diseases are noticeable due to the large amount of water that the dog drinks, which accounts for the constant potty breaks either inside (mistakes) or begging to get outside. I would highly recommend a.s.a.p. a conference about this with your vet.

See - Bladder Stones, Excessive Thirst, and Urinary Tract Infections

Fungus - An irritant usually found in the moist areas on the dog's body. It can be red and very itchy, causing a lot of licking and chewing. Yeast is usually to blame here, so using antifungal creams such as Lotrimin, Lamisil, or Monistat, found in your local drug store, can give relief. Be sure to hold your pet for five minutes to allow the cream to absorb.

A change of diet can make a world of difference too.
See - Butt Draggin', Diet, Eczema,
Feet Lickers, and Yeast Infections

*"Guardian" - the sole protector given the responsibility
to manage the health and well-being
of our loyal companion.*

Gas - Bloating or flatulence. If your dog is bloated, *see
Bloating;* however, flatulence is usually food related.
Definitely look into changing the food if you don't want to live
with the odor. The dog's system is telling you, just as yours
would, that certain foods are not agreeing with its digestion.
Dogs shouldn't have excessive gas, but a few putters are
normal. When the odor permeates the room, action must be
taken.
Change food slowly for starters, but if your family becomes
unconscious, talk to the vet.

Gastric Acid - All who have owned a dog definitely have seen
yellow bile on their carpet, floor, or bed. This is called
gastric acid, also known as stomach bile. Many dogs produce
an overabundance of this acid. Talk to your vet about an
antacid and try to feed three times per day to help absorb
the acid. If you have a picky eater, try soda crackers or a
piece of toast in the morning with the antacid. If the
problem does not subside, especially in middle-aged to elderly
dogs, it could be the sign of a more serious issue. Have your
veterinarian do a blood test to check the liver and kidneys. I
have found in older pets simply changing the dog food to one

with reduced protein, 16% or less can eliminate the vomiting of stomach acid. Just a little helpful hint here: this acid or bile generally gets into the hair and around the mouth of your pet after they have hurled, and it has a very sour smell that you will notice. A bath, at least of their ears and mouth, will be on the things to do list along with shop-vacuuming the carpet.

See - Shop Vac

Giardia - This is otherwise known as Montezuma's Revenge or the trots. Stagnant water is usually where dogs contract it. Bacteria get into your dog's intestines and causes inflammation. Diarrhea, blood in the stool, and possible vomiting result. The smell is vile, and you'll definitely be using the shop vac. This problem is common in dogs during spring and the heat of the summer and should be treated by your veterinarian because dehydration can occur. I recommend Pedialyte or an electrolyte given in the drinking water over the next few days so the poor pooch can build its strength. Your dog may not eat for one to two days, so don't fret. The most important thing is to keep liquids down to promote hydration. When you are ready to reintroduce food, begin with a bland diet given in small amounts.

See - Diet (for recipe) and Shop Vac

Glucosamine - This product is very helpful for the joints. You will find Glucosamine in any pet store in its joint department, sometimes mixed in with MethySulfonylMethane (MSM), Hyaluronic acid, and Chondroitin. We humans take Glucosamine all the time. As a matter of fact, you can give your dog exactly what you are taking; the only difference is the canine type is flavored so your dog will like it. The dosage of human Glucosamine to be used for your dog is: toy/small dogs 200 mg once per day, medium dogs 300 mg once per day, and large dogs 500 mg once per day. You should see results within ten days of using Glucosamine. There are many products on the market today, so if one is not giving you results, by all means try another brand or discuss the issue with your veterinarian.

I like to start very active dogs on Glucosamine when they are one and a half years and up. This will help protect the joints before problems arise.

See – Glucosamine, Hyaluronic Acid and Joints

Grass Eaters - The instant grass starts to sprout, many dogs begin to graze. I find mine like the wider blade types. I don't believe the grass even stays in the dog's stomach more than five minutes before it all comes up and everything is fine again. You can search the web for books until the cows come home, but the reason is unknown why dogs perform this ritual. I don't feel it's harmful, just messy. As the summer progresses, it's not such an issue as everything dries up with the climate. So you can relax now and move right along to the next subject.

See - Shop Vac

Green Beans – These vegetables are the best food substitute to use in reducing your dog's rations in order to decrease body weight. When the decision is made on how much to reduce the dog food, simply add the green beans to substitute for the bulk. For example, when reducing your dog's food by 1/3 cup, add 1/3 cup of green beans as replacement. If more weight needs to be taken off, within a couple of weeks reduce the amount of dog food and repeat with the addition of more green beans. The beans offer good nutrition and fiber not to mention the low caloric intake. You can purchase canned or frozen French cut or whole green beans, whatever suits your fancy. I would suggest buying them in a large can sold in a restaurant supply store and keeping it in the refrigerator for easy use. Then you have it at your fingertips (no excuses). Most dogs will eat these with no argument; however, I'm sure there will be some stubborn, rebellious protesters turning their noses up in disgust. Try to stick with it for seven days, without weakening. Be sure to warm up the beans if you get them out of the refrigerator. Your dog will eat them better. In one month or less, you won't believe the difference you will see in your dog. Its activity and mobility level will surprise you, and the weight melts away easily.

See- Diet, Fatty, Obesity, Overeating

Grooming - I always support grooming your dog; after all, this is a very important part of pet ownership and has become a regular appointment for many a pet owner. If you are capable of washing, cutting, and removing dead hair, I say go for it. You can wash your dog weekly or bi-weekly, but at the very least you should wash the dog once per month. It's simply untrue that washing is harmful to its body oils. If you don't want a smelly house, wash or have your pooch groomed regularly. A shampoo that has a fabulous, lingering smell for days is called Fresh & Clean. It can be purchased at any pet store or online. Be sure that when using this shampoo you leave it on for three to five minutes to allow the fragrance to permeate into the hair. The Fresh & Clean cream rinse is the perfect compliment to the shampoo and maintains the wonderful fragrance throughout your home. Human cream rinse works great too, and I feel for long-haired breeds it has a better detangling quality. Mix the people stuff four parts water to one part cream rinse; otherwise your dog will look greasy. For thirty-five years, I have bathed dogs in human shampoo unless a special shampoo for skin eczema is required. Make sure you rinse, rinse, and rinse again so that all of the soap is out of the dog's hair. Diluting any thick shampoo with water thins the soapy substance and will make rinsing so much easier.

Bathing at home is a common event for many families. Put a rubber bath mat down in the tub to give your pet something to grip while wet and soapy. Teach your dog to sit and be calm without jumping around to avoid a back injury. There is a suction cup tether designed just for bathing and attaches to the wall of you tub or shower. This goes around the neck of your pet and not only keeps it under control but lets you use both of your arms to handle and wash the dog. This must-have item can be found at a larger pet store or in most pet catalogs. Large dogs can be more of a challenge to bathe at home. Dragging them into the tub with all the hair is a pain, and of course you risk that they will jump out and tear through the house all wet and soapy. I advise, in the winter months, those who own a large, hairy dog to take them to a groomer so it can be dried properly and the mess is there and not in your house. In the summer months, bathe your large dog outside with a hose connected to your kitchen sink faucet. Most hardware stores carry adapters that will fit the fixture so you can give your dog a warm instead of cold bath. Starting out with a gentle stream of warm water will help your dog accept the bath much better than a shocking cold hose. I would advise securing your leashed dog to something stable outside and teaching it to sit and stay. Again, a warm bath is so much easier on your dog's skin when you first start, which will help it to accept this ordeal. Be ready: you're going to get a shower too. To get all the dead hair out, use a slicker brush (Ever Gentle Brand or something comparable at any pet store) while the dog is soaped up. This brush grabs a lot of shedding hair and gets it out. Rinse well and continue brushing during this process to finish the job. Get ready: here comes the shaking and your shower. After all the shaking seems to be done, towel your dog off as well as possible; then take your air compressor with a blowing device on the hose and blow the water and rest of the hair off the dog. Do this slowly so as not to frighten your pet. Many large dogs enjoy having the air blown on them. Be cautious around the ears and eyes. There you have it, a big fluffy clean pooch.

Now let us talk about the use of scissors. First, it must be done very, very carefully. If you have a dog with a lot of mats in its hair or hair that is full of burrs, DO NOT cut them out. Nine times out of ten, you will snip your dog's skin by accident. Please let a professional do the job.

Those pet owners who need expert assistance from a groomer should have no trouble finding one. Choose one who accommodates your desire as well as your pet's comfort. Grooming is something your dog will need throughout its life, and you must have a relationship of trust and comfort with your groomer. An excellent groomer will not only professionally cut hair and nails, clean ears and anal glands, but is usually the one who lets you know about any odd findings on your dog's body. Your groomer is up close and personal with that pooch of yours.

By coming in contact with hundreds of dogs, groomers are experts on many health issues and can provide excellent information on skin care, harmful eye injuries, ear infections, allergies, and parasites, not to mention advice on diet, shampoos, great veterinary clinics, safe boarding kennels . . . I could go on and on. After all, a groomer is writing this book.

See - Bathe, Hair, Shampoo, and Shedding Dogs

Growling - This is a way your dog communicates "warning" to you, or a sound it makes in play. You have to be able to determine which type of growl it is. Never, ever tolerate a growl of aggression towards you or your family members. This is a dominant behavior and you should seek the advice of an obedience trainer on how to correct this conduct. The other types of growling: such as playful, warning, and fear, are normal as your dog needs to let you know if it's happy, worried, or on duty watching the home. You will come to learn all the different sounds your dog makes. Always pay attention to other dogs' sounds and body postures for your own safety as well as your dog's well-being.

Gum Color - I think this is something every pet owner should watch and notice. Observe the nice pink color healthy gums have. Pale, whitish gums are an issue to bring to your vet's attention. Also, a dark reddening of the gums above the teeth could be a sign of gum disease. Once again, check with your vet.

See - Teeth

*"Harmony" - the arrangement of positive forces
in the relationship with your dog.*

Hair - Ah, the vanity of it all! All colors, textures, lengths— from straight to wavy to tight curls. Whatever type of hair your dog has, keep it brushed and clean. Pay attention to the look and feel of its coat because this can be an indicator of ill health. Thinning hair around the ears, nose, back, or down the tail could be signs of thyroid problems. Wet hair in an area is a sign for you to check and see what is causing the dog to chew. Fleas could take up residence, creating a very itchy dog that needs your help.

Diet is another important piece of the puzzle here. A better quality dog food always produces healthier hair. There are many additives available to help the skin and coat, so don't be afraid to give them a try. Normally, you should see results within thirty days.

If your dog has long hair, keep the hair cut away from the eyes and rectal area. Springtime is shedding season, when dogs release their winter coats. Matting usually occurs in April through June. You'll wonder what the heck is going on, even after you just brushed your dog's coat and mats appear everywhere in just two days. I refer to this phenomenon as "molting," just like you would see in birds. The dog's body releases its winter coat, and if you don't keep up with it, you'll have a dog whose hair is so matted that the only answer is a close shave. When you have to groom it so close to eliminate the mats, your dog's behavior may change. It may feel naked and bare and sometimes will hide for a few days until it can adjust to the new hairdo. Other dogs may dig at themselves, causing hot spots. The remedy is not to let the matting occur in the first place. During the spring, have your dog groomed a little shorter and more frequently than normal until the shedding season passes. If you have to cut your dog down and it's the sensitive type, I recommend putting a cute t-shirt on it after the haircut. The covering will make the dog feel better until the hair grows in.

See - Grooming and Shedding Dogs

Hair Loss - Hair loss is common in dogs and happens for many reasons. Allergies, fleas, old age, mange, and thyroid imbalance are some reasons that come to mind.

Extreme scratching of the body from allergies or fleas will really cause not only hair loss but redness or possible hot spots. There are related articles for you to read on these subjects in the table of contents.

Old age can be a big factor with hair loss, just as it is for humans. So putting a t-shirt or coat on your dog will help keep it warm.

Rapid hair loss on the ears and muzzle, along with itching, could be a sign your dog has a parasite. Parasites can be picked up in the country where fox and other animals pass this mite on, and it is contagious to other pets your dog comes in contact with.

Slowly thinning hair loss, especially on the back, ears, and bridge of the nose with a black leather look, could be a sign of a poor-functioning thyroid. Your vet can test for all hair loss causes and get your dog back on track with wonderful results.

See - Allergies and Fleas

Harness - The harness is another alternative to control Fido while on a leash or cable. It is a must if your dog has had neck or back injuries. This device is also safer if you use a cable or chain when placing the rascal outside. There are many different types of harnesses available: some to keep your dog from pulling when walking and others that stop the dog from jumping. Select the right harness at the pet store. Most stores are dog friendly with staff ready to help. Do keep a collar on too, if for no other reason than identification. Harnesses should not be worn 24-7 because they will rub raw the areas under the legs. Please pay attention for these possible places of sensitivity.

See - Collars, Identification Tags, and Leashes

Hearing Loss - *See Deafness in Dogs*

Heartworm - The culprit that is a concern to our pets is the mosquito. When your dog is bitten, the heartworm larva is transmitted to the blood and actual long white worms grow all around and through the heart. This is a deadly disease when a preventative is not used. The threat of infection is very high in warm, humid, dense vegetative areas, which are the breeding grounds for the mosquito. Prevention is a must, especially if your dog spends a considerable amount of time outside. The medication is usually in chewable pill form given once a month and most pets love them. However, those that don't love them must be monitored to make sure they actually ingest the medication, or you have not only wasted your money, but you'll have to spend more for treatment to kill the worms if your pet tests positive when checked by your veterinarian. Some dogs are experts at spitting the pill out, or it can get caught in the hair around the mouth and stay there. I feel this is one of the major reasons many dogs that are on the preventative still contract heartworm. So, be very diligent to insure the pill goes down the hatch. As far as whether to give heartworm medication for twelve months or nine months out of the year, it's whatever you prefer. If you live in warmer climates twelve months out of the year, use the medication for twelve months. The cost of this preventative varies with each veterinarian, or you can order them online with a prescription from your veterinarian.

If you find the cost of heartworm treatment through your veterinary clinic to be a financial burden, get on-line at www.ivermectin.com or Google "ivermectin for dogs". The forum located at www.forums2gardenweb.com also provides a lot of helpful information regarding dosage and use. At these sites, you will find a way to protect your pet utilizing the same ingredients for a fraction of the cost. A list of various distributors will be available for you to choose from. If the dosage isn't clear to you, ask your veterinarian for a break-down or contact the manufacturer listed on the product.

Whenever you take on ownership of a dog, there are certain precautions that are worth doing, and this is one of them. If we all use heartworm preventatives for our dogs, it will protect every dog in your neighborhood too.

Heat Cycle - I mean "heat" cycle. The dictionary defines the word as passion and eagerness—so true. The heat cycle happens every six months in dogs over the age of one year. This "blessed" ordeal normally lasts twenty-one days or three weeks. The first seven days begin the process and vaginal bleeding starts (suitors could be hanging outside your door), followed by seven days in estrus (the female will accept the male), and finally during the last seven days the dog is going out of heat. Although the middle seven days are crucial for breeding, this is not always true for every dog, so watch closely for the full three-week period. It is a time that you, as the dog owner, must be very responsible for the comings and goings of your female dog. You could have visitors with four legs coming from miles around. The heat cycle involves a bloody discharge, which can be very messy. Special briefs are sold to help contain the flow and keep your home clean. Some "ladies" (I use this word instead of the B– word) can be a little irritable and uneasy during this time. That is when you pull out the leg irons and chastity belt, along with providing your dog an armed escort to the bathroom. But wait! It soon flip-flops and love begins to fill the air thereafter. Please, please be watchful of your female dog, because there are too many unwanted puppies everywhere. If a mishap occurs, take that little hussy to your veterinarian immediately and get the "bad girl" shot. This "shot" insures that an unwanted pregnancy doesn't occur.

I feel the responsible action as a pet owner is to have your dog spayed or neutered to prevent these unwanted "mishaps". If you spay your female dog before the first heat cycle, you won't have to mess with any of this.

When getting a puppy, most of them will not come into

heat until ten to twelve months old. However, on occasion, the six-month rule holds true.

See - Spaying

Heat Exhaustion - This is a very dangerous state, so pay attention when the hot summers are here. Dark-colored dogs and those with smushed faces and heart conditions can overheat easily. Never leave your pet in the car, even on a warm spring day. A car's interior heats up like a sauna within minutes. I don't recommend even walking your dog in the heat of the summer unless it's early morning or late evening. Keep it cool during the hot days by wetting it down with lukewarm water, give it a kiddy pool, or use a fan if it's kenneled. Some signs of heat exhaustion are: lethargy, disorientation, inability to move, and labored breathing. Things you can do for your dog: cool it down with a cool (not cold) water bath or wrap a cool, wet towel on it. Make sure that you place the cool, wet towel on the belly area between the dog's legs. You will also need to get Pedialyte or an electrolyte fluid into your dog immediately. Use a needleless syringe to give the fluids orally if your pooch will not drink it. The electrolytes will be your dog's savior. If you feel the need to go to your veterinarian, GO.

A good habit to get into is to use electrolytes in your dog's water during the summer or on any occasion it exerts itself. Electrolytes in the powder form are available at any pet supply store or online. This is also a great rule of thumb for hunters to add electrolytes into the dog's water during hunting season.

Heating Pads - NEVER, NEVER use a human heating pad

directly on your dog's body, for burning of the skin can quickly occur. Place a towel between the dog and the pad and monitor the heat—no higher than medium. There are some great thermostatically controlled pads for outdoor doghouses or for heating dog beds. I really like these and recommend them for ensuring your dog's warmth. When using any pad, make sure the cord is in a safe position.

Hematoma - This is a pocket of fluid caused by an injury to the area. A hematoma is common on the flap of a dog's ear. Severe head-shaking from ear infections commonly causes the ears to hit together and the pocket of fluid to build up, but these can occur anywhere on the body. Most people never notice a fat ear until it's really bad. Pay attention to your dog when it shakes its ears repeatedly. If the ears are hot and red, you're on the road to a fat ear. Fido doesn't know to stop aggravating the injury because the ear feels itchy and irritated. I suggest attaching a cone and/or kenneling the dog along with a good dose of Benadryl to calm the feeling. This may take overnight. Always know the amount of Benadryl appropriate for your dog beforehand. Take this seriously: many a dog has had to have an ear surgically slit to stop the fluid from pocketing. If it is not better the next day, see your vet.

See – Cones

Hives - A red rash normally on the belly of the dog means hives. Hives develop from a reaction to food, grass, weeds, shampoos, or insect bites. Benadryl is your friend here. Call your vet to ask about the dosage. A baking soda bath also feels good to your dog. Hives usually go away by the next day.

See - Baking Soda and Welts

Holistic Medicine – Alternative Medicine Veterinarians are becoming very popular all over the country. This philosophy of medicine is proving to be one worth choosing in this changing world of ours. Dysfunction of organs and nerves, metal toxins, and allergies to grains and meat appear more and more often. These doctors practice kinesiology, along with prescribing dietary supplements to balance the body and aid in bringing it back to its rightful functioning. So before you roll your eyes at this idea, do some research. I find holistic treatments to have impressive results, as the body tells its own story.

Honey - This delicious natural wonder is not only very sweet but has been used for many, many years to aid with allergies, diarrhea, coughs, and revitalization in animals. The use of one to two teaspoons a day added to meals or licked right off the spoon is a great way to administer this holistic remedy. It is best to use your local honey, as it has the same pollen in it that affects your pet. Take advantage of the information online.

Hot Spots - What is this? They commonly occur during the summer and fall months. A hot spot is a big red sore that your dog chews or digs on itself. It doesn't know when to quit chewing or digging when creating this lesion. Allergies and fleas are the main reason why the hot spots are formed. However, after being groomed too close on the cheeks or under the chin, some dogs feel chafed, so they start digging

the area. Caution your groomer should you have this happen.
If your dog is prone to hot spots, start the use of Benadryl
and always keep the hair trimmed away from the red areas.
Apply triple antibiotic ointment mixed with a cortisone
cream, which can be found in the drug department of any
store, to the red sore immediately. This helps to heal and
soothe the irritation. Keeping your dog's mouth away from
the hot spot is the quickest way of healing it, so your dog
may have to wear a cone for a while. If you can't get it under
control, see your vet for help.

See - Allergies and Cones

Hugs - Lots and lots of hugs are required for your dog. It
does you just as much good.

Hunched Back - A very common injury that occurs with many,
many dogs is back trauma. A kind of rolled or hunched back
along with the tail hanging down and quiet behavior are
indications that the back is acting up. Once a back injury has
presented itself, you can always plan on a return visit at some
point. Usually baby aspirin (check with the vet for dosage) is
the miracle cure, along with a couple days of rest. Soon you'll
see the tail held up high, and that's the sign all is well. Backs
out of whack can happen a few times a year. Having your
meds ready will help the healing process that much faster.
The good news is most moderate back quirks don't stick
around for long.

See – Back

Hyaluronic Acid – This natural substance is being used with
amazing success in helping dogs and humans suffering from

achy joints or stiffness acquired from old age. When researching joint compounds, make sure there's Hyaluronic acid in the product. My personal research has found that one milligram per pound of weight is the recipe you want to use. The product should contain enough Hyaluronic acid to make a noticeable improvement in your dog's joints. If the product contains less than one milligram per pound of Hyaluronic acid, you won't notice the difference.

See – Arthritis, Glucosamine and Joints

Identification Tags
Immunization
Incontinence
Inheritance
Insurance
Itch

*"Insight" - a clear, internal understanding of
the whole owner-pet relationship*

Identification Tags - If you are a person who helps lost dogs, I'm sure you have found one without identification. This is frustrating for the rescuer. It would be so simple to return the dog to its home if the tags were attached. There are all kinds of identification tags available at the pet stores. If you don't want to buy one, use a sharpie and write your phone number on your dog's collar, PLEASE. When leaving your pet with a friend while you're vacationing, be sure to change the identification tag to one with the friend's address and phone number.

Another wonderful method of identification is the microchip, which is approximately the size of a grain of rice. It's inserted under the skin of your dog and registered nationwide. It's important to always update your personal information in the database, which will keep your pooch's info current if it should become lost. The fee is reasonable and your vet can perform the procedure as well as provide you the necessary information.

Some of the giant department stores have really cool engraving machines in their pet department with very fun tags to choose from. So there's no excuse!

See – Name Tags

Immunization - Absolutely immunize your dog, especially if you socialize it or take it to a groomer, kennel, or dog park. When school starts and you put a bunch of kids together, sickness can occur. This is true with dogs too. Boarding kennels and grooming salons may require immunization verification in order to protect all other dogs entering the business. Kennel cough is one vaccine I think should be given every six months if you board your dog frequently. I don't feel dogs are protected well after ten months into the vaccination. Some dogs have reactions to various vaccinations, so pay attention to your dog and remind your veterinarian about any reaction the next time your dog goes in for shots. Also, have all of your shots given in the spring when you go in for heartworm testing. This will save you additional trips to the veterinarian during the year.

See - Vaccines

Incontinence - Wetting the bed (leaking urine while asleep) is one form of incontinence. I have seen this occur in young dogs; however, it tends to be a geriatric matter. If wetting happens while your dog is asleep, be glad because there is a solution. Let your veterinarian know it only happens while the dog is sleeping, and he/she will know the right meds to give. However, if you are finding puddles on your floor, you could be dealing with old age or another medical condition. Old age wetting can be helped by crating your dog when you're not able to be at home. Giving the dog freedom allows it to go potty in the house and get away from the mess, but if confined, it will not like going potty where it lays. So usually crating stops this problem. If you notice puddles occurring at night, try leashing the dog to your bed. Once again, it will

not want the mess in its area. An overabundance of drinking and wetting should be discussed with your veterinarian.
See - Excessive Thirst

Inheritance - Otherwise known as genetics. When you buy a puppy, especially an expensive breed, you have the absolute right to see both parents. Look at the ears, skin, personality, confirmation, and if possible take someone who knows about dogs and behavior to help you decide. Many people buy a dog on impulse and have a lifetime of medical traumas. I cannot stress enough that the parents' personality and health can tell you a lot about the puppy you pick.

Insurance - I'm not a person fond of insurance. I can't understand why people pay pet insurance companies money each month but cannot set up a savings account for their dog with the same discipline. Placing $30 to $40 per week or month in an account designated for your dog is a nice little nest egg for Rover. At some point in your dog's life you will need the funds for medical reasons, and if not, the money is yours.

Itch - *See Allergy, Cones, Diet, Hot Spot, Mange, Staph Infection, and Yeast Infections*

J

INDEX

Jogging
Joints
Jumping

*"Joy" - the indescribable happiness received
from unconditional love.*

Jogging - If you're a jogger (and I'm certainly not), try doing this activity with your dog. It's a wonderful energy burner for your four-legged friend. Be aware of other dogs on your running path so you can both enjoy a great workout without a dog confrontation. It is not a bad idea to carry a small can of pepper spray in unfamiliar regions. Start your dog jogging with you a little at a time to allow their joints and pads of the feet to get acclimated to running. I would also suggest avoiding hot pavement as they can get their pads burned. After a good jog with your dog, invite it to drink water that has been enhanced with an electrolyte formula to aid with hydration.

See - Walking

Joints - Take good care of your dog's joints. There are excellent supplements available, and they can be started as early as two years old for large dogs that are extremely active. With respect to all producers of joint complex additives, I hear wonderful reviews from a company called Ramard Inc. They not only offer compounds for dogs, but also people and first and foremost for horses, www.ramardinc.com. Now, those big beasts *really* wear on their joints, which lead me to believe that this company knows joints. Why I feel so strongly about this company's product is it contains a supplemental ingredient called Hyaluronic acid. This product contains higher doses than most other joint compounds I've encountered. The use of a soft thick bed is also a necessity so your dog is not lying on a hard floor. A baby bed mattress (which can be picked up at a garage sale) with a cover is excellent for large dogs. Become weight conscious because excess weight will wear on the joints more than anything else.

See – Arthritis, Glucosamine and
Hyaluronic Acid

Jumping - "Boing," "Boing," "Boing." Enough already. Some breeds are natural born jumpers. It can be very funny and also annoying. Large dogs love to jump up and greet you with a big lick-a-roo. If you let it start, it is a hard habit to break. If you don't like it, don't encourage it. Make sitting the greeting mode. Many, many leg injuries are caused when jumping occurs, from the knees to the ligaments, and let's not forget the back. Especially as your dog ages and puts on weight, I recommend discouraging the jumping.

Sleeping with your furry friend is great, but teach it from the start that you will lift it onto the bed (if it's a small dog) instead of allowing your dog to jump up. This little cuddly beast will learn to wait for you to pick it up. Another good idea is the stairs or ramps sold for dogs can be use when placed by the bed or furniture. I have seen it work and with a little training your dog will be running up and down the stairs or ramps instead of jumping. Teaching a young dog to use them right from the start is a wise decision, because it will never develop the jumping habit. If you think this is silly

SO WHAT DO I KNOW?!

Advice, ask your veterinary clinic how many of these injuries they treat each year.

See – Back and Knees

Kenneling
Kids
Kisses
Knees

"Karma" – what goes around comes around;
what you give you get.

Kenneling – This is a big subject for many pet owners. I am an advocate of training your dog via a kennel. However, there are people out there who still think it is cruel to contain your dog in a kennel/crate. I can only say that those folks who do not believe in crating better not dare complain when their dog doesn't potty train, chews their cupboards or walls, digs their carpet up, chews an electrical cord, eats something deadly, or finds that couch cushion a afternoon of fun.
All dogs will get bored when they are young and left unattended for hours. Kenneling your dog gives it security and calmness as well as giving you peace of mind and a full pocketbook.

   With a young dog, kenneling should occur even if you are home all day and not able to keep watch over them. These are the reasons why:

   1. A puppy needs down time or a nap;
   2. You need the down time;
   3. It allows the dog to learn to be alone;
   4. It teaches your dog the concept of confinement when it goes to the veterinarian or travels via air/car;
   5. A puppy will potty train faster;
   6. It provides safety; and

7. It gives you a place to keep your pet when you have company or workmen in your house.

Remember, these wonderful creatures are not people, and we can control the home and their lives while they are with us. As your dog gets older, you can start to trust it a little at a time. Test this with short trips to the store and always reward the good behavior. But never stop kenneling your dog. I realize that with a big dog the cage is a pain in the behind, but a nice spot in your basement or a spare bedroom is ideal. As your dog ages, it will need confining again due to incontinence. If you do not keep kenneling familiar it will reject it later in life. Then, when confinement is necessary the rebellion with non-stop barking and digging is likely to happen. I've come up with some rules you might want to follow:

Rule #1: Never release your dog from the kennel when it is barking to get out, because this is a surefire way to start cage anxiety. Make the release under your terms, and not until the dog is quiet.

Rule #2: Teach the puppy that the kennel is its home and a wonderful place to sleep/rest. It is in the best interest for you and your dog. Feed it in the kennel from the start so your dog goes in and out freely. This will make the expectations of kenneling a given for your dog.

Rule#3: Never allow any barking or digging in the kennel. Give a very firm command word of your choice and cover the kennel with a sheet. Having to repeat the voice command in the training days is common. Don't give up!

Rule#4: Leave the dog in the cage after you arrive home for a few minutes to calm down. Do not speak to the dog until you open the door. This will allow you to be in control and release the dog under your terms.

Metal versus plastic: I have used both types, and I like the plastic kennel the best. I have seen too many dogs try to bite the metal cage, and they get their teeth caught up in the wire. When this happens, the dog goes wild with panic and squealing, possibly breaking a tooth in the process. The plastic kennel is cozy, offering the dog a sanctuary. The downside of a plastic kennel is they are hotter during the summer months, so run a fan. If you start a young dog in a metal cage, generally there is not a problem. The damage happens if the dog has never been crated before. Always monitor a new dog for safety purposes. We want our dog to love and enjoy its home, not to be fearful of it. If you notice anxious behavior, get help right away to stop and soothe this frantic action.

See - Anxiety, Cage Anxiety, and Puppies

Kids - This can be a wonderful mixture with a dog or a complete disaster. Kids can learn wonderful life skills taking care of their pet. This teaches them responsibility for another living creature. Feeding, bathing, walking, and cleaning up the yard is all part of pet ownership. Parents play a huge role in teaching and displaying pet duties. Kids are kids and tend to forget the everyday stuff once the newness has worn off, so it's the grown-ups' job to keep them motivated. Please do not let your kids or their friends tease the dog when it is young. Your dog will never forget it. Furry little creatures are so irresistible to kids, and they want to squeeze them, love them, hold them, and walk around with them. Before you can even blink, your little, teeny weenie puppy has been dropped on the ground. I cannot tell you how often this occurs. With a puppy, have the kids sit on the ground while cuddling it. This will create a safe area for the puppy and give the child freedom to hold and love it.

Now let's talk about the danger kids can be in. Teach your kids to be confident around dogs but cautious. Remember that kids are at eye level to large dogs, and this requires your close supervision. Never trust a dog you do not know to be face to face with your child. Kids are very quick, and these quick movements bother some dogs that are not around youngsters all of the time. Have your kids walk instead of run around dogs, which will make a difference in how dogs react. Teach them never to run up to a dog they don't know, but to admire from a distance. Above all things, teach your kids to love and respect all creatures.

Kisses - What creature does not like this act of affection? A kiss is better than Milk Bones any day. Please, make a habit of kissing your dog. It is my promise to you that it will return the love to you tenfold.

Knees - Certain breeds have knee problems right from the get go. Many toy breeds struggle with knee caps that move in and out. Weight, weight, weight is the secret recipe for the knees. Your veterinarian can tell if your dog's knees pop at a young age. I recommend minimal running and no jumping to preserve the dog's knees and to avoid surgery.
See – Diet, Glucosamine, and Joints

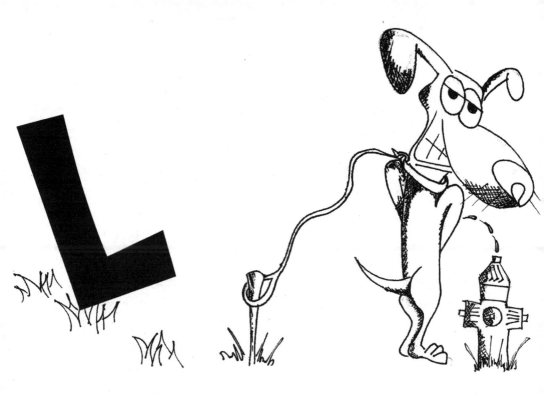

*"Love" - the most elevated emotion on earth
to be shared with all living creatures.*

Leashes - I have seen a variety of leashes in my days. From a person's belt to a shoe string, and how about a bathrobe tie or a horse lead? Come on people, let's buy a half dozen leashes and keep them in each car, coat closet, coat rack, wherever. Become creative and make leashes—you don't have to spend a lot of money on material. Think about it: your kids, who love arts and crafts, can make a leash for the dog. I love the extension leashes where a dog can walk, and the leash recoils all by itself. When in training, your instructor may recommend a certain type of leash, usually leather, which works best for control.

It's always smart to have an extra leash in your car for those times of rescue, or if the car should break down while the dog is with you. Leashes go along with the First Aid Kit, an absolute must.

Owning a dog that chews the leash can become not only annoying, but expensive too. They can gnaw right through that thing in a couple of minutes, even while you stopped to talk to your neighbor. Then the chase begins. There is only one leash that will fix this particular problem and that is a chain leash. Your dog will learn in a hurry that there is no escaping this one.

Training a puppy to accept a leash should be on the "to

do" list, and it is quite easy. Start by attaching a lightweight leash to its collar in the house, letting the puppy drag the leash around. Every so often, pick up the leash and walk around the house with it. It won't take much time at all before your dog recognizes the leash as a fun thing. Also, dogs should learn to go potty on a leash (*See Catching of the Urine*) as well as off the leash.

Another helpful hint, if you volunteer to take care of someone's dog at your house, remember it does not know your house or yard or smells. Typically, it can take a couple of days for the dog to feel comfortable in your surroundings, so keep the leash on it for the dog's protection. Feeling nervous in your home may cause it to try to bolt out the door and run to find its home. At least if the visiting dog is dragging a leash, you will be more likely to catch it, and, psychologically, the dog thinks you are in control.

Owning a dog that is a runner cannot only be aggravating, but a real challenge. These pooches are so full of life, all they can think about is freedom. Here's a way you can give it some independence in the yard: Get a twenty-foot leash or rope and tie one end to a laundry detergent bottle full of water (this could be three or four bottles if you have a larger dog; use your best judgment, even with smaller dogs); use a harness instead of a collar so the dog will not pull on its neck. Hook up the other end of the rope to the harness and let your dog run around the yard. Dragging the bottles gives the dog a weight or anchor to limit the roaming, yet it provides some liberty for them to explore.
Remember, you may need to fill the bottle more or empty some water according to the dog's size and weight.

Many of our furry friends have a sixth sense about

knowing when you're going to the veterinarian or groomer, and they slither off to hide under the bed or even snap at you. No problem: attach the leash to its collar the evening prior or in the morning. Your dog will come right along with you. Two can play at this game, and the leash always wins.
See - Runaways

Leg Lifters - This topic is not about lifting the leg to urinate; it is the constant lifting and marking that becomes a really bad habit. I find dogs that are leg lifters tend to be dominant by nature. Marking of territory here and there, on your clothing, on your couch, kitchen cupboards, wherever. You can't take your dog to anyone else's home because no one wants them to visit. I hate to say it, but most of the problem is your fault. You have to stop this behavior right away. For example, if you take your male dog (or female because she will do it too) on a walk and allow it to urinate every two minutes, you are encouraging the marking. You need to train it to empty its bladder all at once and never allow marking. A walk is just that: a walk. Lead your dog along and tell it "no." It will learn what you want it to learn. In the case of taking "Fido" to the relative's home, do your family a favor and watch your dog. Keep it on a leash or have it wear a wrap in the home. You will see that others are more likely to embrace your dog if they see you respect their home by being watchful of where your pet is roaming. Take a kennel along too. Some dogs will never stop leg lifting in others' homes, so don't feel insulted if your friends don't want you to bring your dog over to their house.
See - Wee Wee Wrap

Legs - The legs are the most vital limbs. They take so much abuse, and they log uncountable miles over the life of your dog. By keeping your dog fit and trim, you can prolong joint health. Do not overwork these fabulous appendages by excessive walking or running. Massage them for your dog. You will find it loves this. Legs of very small dogs and puppies can be easily broken, so when you are unable to watch them, a child's playpen is an ideal way to keep them safe.

Lethargy - This is when your pooch has no "get up and go." Lethargy usually is an indication of feeling ill, a lack of energy, or dehydration. One day of this you can handle at home by ensuring your dog is getting an energy drink even if you have to syringe it into its mouth. If this problem persists for a couple of days, see your veterinarian. Dogs are not like humans, and making up an illness to get a day off of work is highly unlikely. Dogs have a wonderful ability to love life and live in the moment. So when your dog is out of sorts, something could be brewing.

See - Pedialyte

Licking – Oh, what a habit this is, and are we glad we do not do it. There are a lot of reasons behind this licking thing: show of affection, an indication of a problem in the area being licked, a method of cleaning, or simply that the motion provides tranquility and soothing. Watch where the licking takes place to easily identify what is bothering your dog, if anything. If the licking is constant, investigate because the skin can become irritated from excessive licking.

A dog's cleaning of its private area is very common; however, powerful or constant licking in this area could be an indication of an irritation, infection, or the heat cycle (for females). Be sure to see your veterinarian when the licking involves this area. Obsessive licking causing redness must be stopped, usually with a cone. If we don't help our dog stop, it won't, and the licking can turn into a much bigger problem in the future. Sour sprays are available to give the area a bad taste, and repetitive treatments may be necessary to avoid licking that spot. A method that I have used to stop licking is called screaming at it. This only gets your blood pressure up but doesn't stop the licking so seek other methods. Don't be grossed out if your dog likes to lick you, your face, your feet, your hands. This is a sign of pure love and affection.

See – Cones, Hair Loss, and Hot Spots

Limping - The gimpy walk has an array of possibilities attached to it, ranging from a broken toenail to a broken toe, or a popping knee to a torn ligament, or a broken leg. Let us not forget the hips or a laceration of some type as well. Always check your pet's toes by touching them, or the nails. They will let you know when the area is sensitive.

If the nail has been torn off, clean the area with peroxide and put triple antibiotic cream on. Place gauze and the stretch bandage over the area, but don't wind it too tightly. Remember, your dog will try to chew the bandage off, so use the cone.

If the limp is in the back leg, and your dog is using the foot, you can wait a few days. During that time, give your dog some baby aspirin in the a.m. and p.m. Usually, the problem will get better. No exercise during this time; let the leg rest until normal use returns. If the limp persists, see your veterinarian. You must remember: weight is very important with any leg injury.

Love - Love, love, love, I know you're singing the Beatles song along with me. This is an easy one, and it is one of the most important elements of pet ownership. What you give to your dog you will get in return. I will leave you with this beautiful quote that was on a sign I purchased: "Your dog is the only one that loves you more than he loves himself." So, so true.

Lumps - Lumps and bumps and marble-like cysts are very common on every dog starting around six years old. Most of them that you feel under the skin are fatty tumors, which are not a worry but do look bothersome. Always ask your vet about them when you are in for a check-up, and he/she will ease your mind. Some dogs tend to be lump producers, and they start popping up all over. Or the ones that have become large and cumbersome. Removal is always an option and is beneficial in some cases. Pay attention to your dog's body and the location and size of lumps, so you can point them out during a doctor visit.

See – Fatty Tumors

INDEX

Mange
Massage
Money
Motion Sickness
Multiple Dogs
Murphy's Law
Music

"Motivation" - the personal tool recommended for accomplishing the end results in your partnership between man and beast.

Mange - This terrible affliction could be another reason for hair loss and itching. Mange is caused by a tiny mite that gets under the skin, creating a world of scratching. There are many different types, some contagious to humans. If you suspect this or would just like to be on the safe side, have your veterinarian do a skin scraping to ease your mind. There are very successful treatments to heal your pet. Get online and read—there is so much information to help you understand this subject.

See – Hair Loss and Itch

Massage - Close your eyes and imagine the feeling of being massaged. The low soothing music, the warm towels, the smell of lavender oil . . . okay, wake up. I am talking about our dogs now. Your dog will love it as much as we do. There probably won't be a need for music or oil, but a good and loving rub down puts your dog in such a tranquil state. Just watch the silly faces when you massage it and how relaxed and content it becomes. I better stop this kind of talk; it is making me too tranquil. Try it and you will see. And NO, I don't have a 900 number for you.

Money – Oh, what a powerful word! We all have it, use it, hoard it, and spend it. Money usually buys the dog you have and is used to take care of that dog. Plan, plan, plan for and save money for your pet. There is no excuse why you can't. We plan for the car, we plan for a vacation, we plan for dinner and a movie, and we plan for a lot of family issues. But when it comes to our dog that loves us, makes us laugh, comforts us, preserves our well-being, shows us undying loyalty, we come up with all kinds of excuses about spending money on our most trusted companion. We all know ahead of time that there are yearly expenses. So save for it. If you travel and board your dog, budget it into your vacation expenses. Once you get into the saving habit, which you should practice weekly, you will enjoy not worrying about how you will pay for pet expenses when they occur. Hands off, do not touch this money for anything but dog stuff. That is called discipline.

See – Insurance and Savings Account

Motion Sickness - How many of us have traveled with a roll of paper towel in the car just to be prepared for our pets' queasy stomach? Many dogs get sick while traveling in a car, from young puppies to full-grown adult dogs. You can see it in their eyes, then the mouth starts to salivate, and before you have gone five miles the car needs cleaning. The odd thing is, usually the dog wants to go with you in the car.

There are medications your vet can give you, and I have used over-the-counter motion sickness pills with great success. You should check with your vet for the correct dosage according to the weight of your dog. Try to give the pills two hours before the car trip. You can help your dog overcome this affliction if you will spend some time every day for just ten minutes driving around the block with your dog, but no farther, and when you arrive home, take the dog on a walk. The minute a dog with this tendency gets into the car, it already has become nerved up. If you show the dog that a ride is a fun experience, I think you will be very shocked with the results. You have to get its mind off of vomiting and onto fun—the walk. As the dog responds positively, drive further until you're up to thirty minutes, and so on. But until you have mastered this event, keep the paper towels in the car.

See – Shop Vac

Multiple dogs - This is so darn common these days, families that have two to four dogs. Let me first say that I have been a multiple dog owner for many years, so I feel a little bit like a "know it all" on the subject. The first reason people own multiple dogs is to give their dog a companion. The second reason may be because they want another dog. The third reason, I feel, is to save the poor homeless dog that no other person could care for like they can. I have been down that road too many times to count.

Is it a good idea? Well, here are some words of advice:

1. Take in only as many dogs as you can afford.
2. Realize it's a long commitment.
3. Ask yourself, is there time to spend with each of the dogs?
4. Remember, travel is harder with more than one dog.
5. The pack mentality can occur with multiple dogs, so what will you do about it?

6. Agreement between all family members about taking additional dogs is vital because more dogs mean more confusion, noise, and work.

7. Make sure you have one dog completely trained and behaving well before involving another. Bad habits can rub off on the newcomer. If you want more in another year, go for it.

8. If your house is already wild with excitement due to kids, I would highly discourage multiple dogs. Please, do not put another dog into your home in an attempt to fix other household issues then end up placing the dog elsewhere. This doesn't teach our kids much about the concept of commitment. It also adds to the negative problems already close to eruption.

9. Consult your veterinarian or an animal behaviorist regarding the safe number of pets that should occupy one home. You want a balance of harmony in your kingdom. If this balance is not maintained, you will experience behavioral problems from the dogs, like fighting and potty problems.

10. Always remember, we get our pets to enhance our lives, not to cause more havoc.

See – Savings Account

Murphy's Law - This is exactly why I am preaching about saving money. There isn't a person I know who hasn't had a visit from Murphy. It always visits after hours or on a holiday, Saturday night or Sunday morning. We can make

Murphy's joyous surprises more of a calm arrival if we are prepared. Please be prepared with common sense thinking, a savings account for your pets, and a first aid kit, along with phone numbers to your vet placed in a visible spot.

Music - Music has a magic all its own. There are quite a few Music CDs online for the listening ears of our pooches. Check it out. Play the radio when you're at work or gone for the evening. You'll find a very relaxed pet when you get home.

*"Nurture" - the tender care that fosters
the love to promote the relationship.*

Nails - They can scratch the heck out of you if you're not careful. Nails could easily be nipped every two weeks. Learn how with a good pair of clippers and some blood stop in case you cut too much off. Just take off 1/8 inch or so, and then use a big emery board to file them. It's really not a big deal for you to do this on your own. Even filing the nails weekly is okay. If you can't do this, take your dog to the groomer or vet for a nail trim. Nails that are too long can break off, leaving your dog in a lot of pain as well as a bloody mess in the house. Very few dogs are exercised enough to wear down their nails where they should be, so please try to trim or have them trimmed at least monthly.

Name Tags - It is our responsibility to make sure our pet has identification on it at all times. If you don't like the jingling of tags, then buy a collar with the name and phone number embroidered on it. Name tags come in assorted shapes and colors, and they can be made up on the spot at most pet stores. I recommend the engraved name tags because they are legible and water-proof.

If you travel to a summer home or lake home, have the proper tags for this area too. Also, if someone is going to be taking care of your pet at their home, have a tag made with the pet-sitter's address and phone number so the dog can be returned to them if it should get away. Some dogs chew on the tags, making them bent and scratched. Check the tags occasionally to see if the address and phone number are still legible.

See - Identification Tags

Nearsightedness - Do dogs need corrective glasses? Well, the truth is many dogs struggle with nearsightedness or (myopia). Certain breeds have a tendency towards this more than others. Retrievers, Cocker Spaniels, Springer Spaniels, Rottweilers, and German Shepherds have been recognized to be the breeds most likely prone to nearsightedness. Studies show that genetics play a major role in passing on this condition. So if you notice your dog doesn't quite see where you threw the ball, you're probably right. At least you can rest assured it has nothing to do with intelligence.

See - Eyes

Neck Injury - Grabbing the stuffed toy and shaking it to death over and over and over is a great way to cause a neck injury. It's instinctive for Fido to shake the dickens out of anything in the dog world, but don't let it go too far. You won't see the damage for a couple of years until your dog ages, but it will happen. Collars are another neck damager. If long walks or runs are in store, select a harness and use the collar for identification.

Raising the food and water bowls will help with any spine injury. In fact, it's a good idea to feed and water from raised bowls to prevent injury.

Neuter – Snip, snip here, snip, snip there, and a couple of la de das. Oh yes, I'm all for this type of surgery for our "little boy" dogs. I like to see the owners wait until the pup is six to seven months old. My rule is when the adult teeth have come in, schedule the surgery. The reason for waiting is many toy breeds do not lose all their baby teeth and they need to have them pulled. So why not pull teeth while your pet is sedated for neutering? This surgery helps prevent prostate issues later in your dog's life, helps with potty and behavioral issues, and just all around calms your dog down so it can focus on what you want instead of what's going on in its mind.

After surgery, it is a good idea to keep a watchful eye on your dog so it doesn't lick or chew at the incision site. Keep a cone close at hand so you can use it when necessary during the times you cannot closely watch your dog. It only takes a short period of time before your dog chews open the site, so pay very close attention. This may not happen immediately after the procedure, but as the sutures dry and begin pulling, it may cause the dog to start licking.

Will your precious furball gain weight? Only if you don't monitor the food. Is it a better dog for your family if neutered? I believe in my heart it is.
See – Cones and Teeth

Nicknames - Every dog I've ever owned has had about ten different names and responds to each one. Can you change the name if you are adopting? Absolutely, just use the old name along with the new for a few days, and then drop the old. You'll be amazed how fast it responds.

Nose - And what a sensitive appendage this nose is. A tracking device like no other. I don't believe there is a piece of scientific equipment yet that can trace scent like the nose of a dog. With all that sniffing, nasal flair-ups are common in dogs too. The more smushed the face and nose, the more problems. Excessive sneezing usually happens during allergy season along with those crazy backward sneezes. Ask your vet about an antihistamine to help control the nose thing. However, repetitive sneezing in older animals could be a signal that something medical is brewing. There are tests that can be performed to see what the trouble is. Some breeds tend to get a raised crust that starts forming on the top ridge of the nose around eight years old and up. A common development in Cockers, it can cover the whole nose and become very sensitive with pieces that come off, leaving raw flesh underneath. There are ointments at most animal clinics to help clear this up, but it takes your diligence in applying the ointment in order for it to work.

A lot of noses change color. Causes for this can be climate, use of plastic dishes for food and water, and I believe that some dogs just have a different kind of skin pigment. If your dog spends a lot of time outside and has a pinkish-colored nose, check with your local pet store for an available sun block.

There shouldn't be drainage from the nostrils, especially with a yellow or green color to it. This is an indication of an infection, meaning you need to go to the doggie doctor.

Noses usually are moist and cool to the touch; however age tends to dry things up, so it is not uncommon for older dogs to have a dry nose.

> *See - Allergies, Backward Sneeze, and Cocker Nose*

"Optimism" - the part of your mind that knows all will be well.

Obedience Training - Great idea! I find it very helpful, for the owner more so than the dog in some cases. Check with your local vet, pet store, or phone book for trainers in your area and also the type of obedience you want to accomplish. These classes are fun and very rewarding but require you to follow through and continue the training daily in order to reap the results you want. Practice your obedience lessons in your home or while on walks. There are many superb books in the animal section of all major bookstores that will provide even more knowledge. The National Geographic Channel and the Animal Planet have first-hand, world-renowned, mega-skilled trainers for you to watch and learn from right before your very eyes. Give obedience training some consideration, even with older pets.

Obesity - This subject goes hand in hand with the topic "Overeating." This is a huge problem with people and pets today. There are so many wonderful treats packaged to catch our eye when we stroll through the doggy aisle at any store. So we proceed to feed them their breakfast and many treats throughout the day, then of course supper and part of our supper, some popcorn, ice cream, and who knows what else. Why are we doing this to ourselves and our pets? I can harp and harp on all the health issues that we have already heard about, with a very small percentage of owners willing to take charge. Obesity blows knees out, harms backs, and causes major health complications just like humans experience. Take control by measuring a limited amount for the day. Watch your dog's body: look for a nice shape and monitor it often, changing the amount of food by an increase or decrease if needed. Adjust food amounts by 1/3 more or less according to their weight. Most all of your vet clinics will let you weigh your pet, so you can watch the improvement.

As your dog ages, it will shock you how little food is needed to maintain the proper pounds. I am not fond of the self-feeding method, simply because you can't plan on a certain amount being eaten. Offering meals twice a day is best in my opinion, with limited small treats in between. Green beans, lettuce, carrots, and apple pieces are great low-cal treats to offer. You the owner have created a habit in your pet to beg all day long. It's time to take charge and change the habit to playing ball or going for a walk. This will help both of you.

See - Diet, Exercise, Fatty, Overeating, Self-Feeding, and Stubborn Eaters

Oral Care - Just because they are dogs doesn't mean they shouldn't have their teeth brushed. As a matter of fact, it is highly recommended to do just that. Dog toothbrushes and toothpaste are sold widely, along with all kinds of products developed especially for oral care. Keep track of how white your dog's teeth are, and the smell of its breath and color of the gums. It's very important for the health of your dog to do so. A product that I highly recommend you purchase is from an online company called Oxyfresh. They offer several wonderful oral care products that give your pooch incredibly fresh breath and clean teeth. I would suggest their Pet Oral Hygiene Solution, and I know you won't be sorry. Just adding it to their water will astound you. www.oxyfresh.com or #1-800-333-7374

See - Bad Breath and Teeth

Outdoor Dog Pens - How you take care of and display your outdoor dog pen shows those who see it what type of character you have. Keeping the pen neat and clean, warm, and shaded reflects well on you. Remember to use straw for bedding in the winter as well as a heated water bowl. Use tarps to protect your dog from the wind and provide shade. Also, imagine yourself in this pen. Take the dog out daily for a change of scenery and exercise. I understand that a dog needs a place to be when we can't watch it or be with it, but I too often see the pen becoming a prison for your pet.

See - Doghouses

Overeating - I am very guilty of this right along with all of my dog friends. Many, many dogs just don't have a clue when to stop eating. Gluttony in the first degree! You, the owner of this beast, must take control of the food. Give measured amounts and that's that. Will they beg? Yes! But don't feed them; you will be promoting the habit. Give a chew toy or the "no" command. These dogs have a bottomless pit, and it's up to us to regulate it. These types of dogs are always in search of any morsel they can find and continually surf the counter for any meager crumb. Try out these helpful tips:

Rule 1: Don't allow the dog in the kitchen,

Rule 2: Keep the counter free and clean of food.

Rule 3: Use child-proof locks so your dog can't get into the cupboards.

Rule 4: The trash bin must be in a locked cupboard and change the bag often.

Rule 5: Store the dog food in a lockable plastic container on a high shelf, in a closet, or in the garage.

How do I know all these tricks? From living with food obsessive dogs. Unless you are very strict with your dog and follow Rule 1, the food-oriented pet is hard to break.

It's easy to simply tolerate the behavior. Think ahead for your own sanity in the home. After taking the time to cook a beautiful family meal, leave it on the counter for just a minute, and whoops, there goes the pot roast. Whose fault will it be? Putting your dog in its kennel while making a meal will keep the peace at home.

See - Diet, Fatty, Obedience Training, Obesity, Self-Feeding, and Stubborn Eaters

*"Patience"- the ability to persevere calmly
in the face of difficulties.*

Pads - The pads on the foot of a dog take an immeasurable amount of abuse. Can you just imagine everything the pads touch and are exposed to? Hot sidewalks or pavement, sharp stones and gravel, dry weeds in the fall, cold snow in the winter. They really do need shoes. Pay attention to hot pavement in the summer as well as low temps in winter. There are great products for hunting dogs to apply to the pads and protect them when you head out to the fields. Boots can be purchased for winter too, but it takes some practice before the dog accepts them. During the hot, humid summer months, chewing of the pads could become a constant event. Very red and inflamed skin all around the pad is usually a sign of a fungus that is as itchy as poison ivy. Treat these areas with an antifungal cream, and when the cold weather arrives you'll notice the skin heals.

*See – Allergies, Fungus, and Yeast
Infections*

Panting - We all know this one. The mouth is open, tongue out, dripping drool. There are many reasons that dogs pant, but the most common is to cool themselves. Panting provides a way to release heat from their bodies. Anxiety, along with feelings of fear or excitement, also causes panting. Don't get upset; it's just what dogs do. However, if your dog is panting to the extreme, ask your vet about it. You'll be able to sense if it's abnormal. Also, watch the heat and get your dog into a cool place during the summer months along with a lot of water. Throw some ice cubes into the water too.

Patience - This is one of the most important qualities a pet owner can practice. Be understanding and calm, for patience always prevails in the end. In this world we live in, patience isn't something we practice as much as we should. However, it's good for our health and our interactions with others. This is truly a positive action. Give it a try.

Paw Wax - This product can be purchased at a pet store or through a pet catalog to help the older dog from sliding on the floor. It also can be used for hunting dogs in the field. Directions are given on the package as to how much, when, and how often to use this product.

Pedialyte - I've used this many times with sick or under the weather dogs. You find it in the baby aisle of the grocery store. It's a pick-me-up to boost the body. Put it in the water bowl or just squirt it with a needleless syringe into the dog's mouth. It's wonderful to use in the hot summer or if you have had a long day hunting with your dog.

> *See – Diarrhea, Giardia, Heat Exhaustion, Lethargy, and Vomiting*

Pills - There will be a time in your dog's life that pills are required. Some dogs just swallow them and others . . . not so much. You can hide pills in anything soft and edible like peanut butter, cheese, meat spread, canned dog food, or a product called "pill pockets" that can be purchased at any pet store.   These marvelous little goodies are excellent for disguising any pill your dog needs to ingest. The important thing is that you, as the pill giver, must witness it going down the hatch and make sure it's not left hanging on the pooch's beard or spit up onto the floor. Do not just put the pill in your dog's food unless you watch that it is actually ingested.

Many dogs acquire heartworm because the owner faithfully gives the pill but does not watch to be sure that it was eaten. This will leave your dog unprotected. Believe me, dogs can become experts at eating the goods and removing the pill. For smaller breeds, many vets can conjure up a compound in liquid form, similar to what we give our children, and you use a dropper or needleless syringe to give the meds.

Pimples - Pimples spotted on the belly or under the front legs, down the top of the head traveling to the back, or really anywhere in groups usually is an indication of a staph infection. Lots of digging and itching are part of this also. You have to take a trip to your animal clinic for some antibiotics to clear this up. It will keep spreading if you don't. Having the hair cut short and treating with a medicated shampoo will be part of this healing process.

See – Acne, Staph Infection, and Zits

Poisons - If your dog is sick and you think or know it has gotten into a dangerous substance, call this number for advice: 1-888-426-4435 or 1-900-680-0000. See the Appendix for a list of foods and plants that are poisonous to your beloved pooch.

Poop - What a word! What we describe as poop is not even close to the dictionary's description. Oh well, that's our language for yah. On this subject, know when, watch the occurrences during training, and keep an eye on what it looks like. We do for ours, so watch your dog's. You might find some really interesting lost articles in this substance, possibly something worth retrieving. I'm sure there are plenty of stories. Make certain there is a very clean path for the poop to drop off the dog's fanny. Pick up all poop in the yard. You wouldn't want to walk in yours and neither does your dog. I use a one-gallon pail with a plastic spoon and wrist-putt the waste product into the pail. It's easy as pie. This is a must, especially if you own multiple dogs. What you feed your dog can govern how much of the stuff you'll be picking up. The less filler in the food, the less poop to pick up.

Have your vet test the stool yearly for parasites when you have the annual check-up.

See – Diarrhea, Giardia, and Soft Stool

Poop Eaters - Yum yum, I don't think anyone has a reason for this disgusting behavior. Any breed from toy to large can be a poop eater. I've had the privilege of owning a few dung hounds myself. It is said your dog can look and act like the owner. Well, I recycle products in my home, so maybe my dog wants to recycle too. Just a thought. There are pills on the market and you can also put hot pepper or Tabasco sauce on the poop, but I find picking it up works best. There is an enzyme called Prozyme that does seem to work if you blend it on the dog's food daily. The Prozyme is supposed to stop the craving for poop, theirs or others'. It can't hurt to try it.

Now, you might own a poop eater that only eats other dogs' poop or cat poop. I gate my cat litter off, so that takes care of that problem, or you can put your cat's litter in a really big Rubbermaid container with a snap-on lid. Then, cut a hole in the top lid large enough for the cat to get into. Eureka! Instant cat-poop proof. I notice winter is a season for a lot of dogs to eat it. I guess they want a poopsicle. I'll pass on that.

Potty Training - This topic is the number one complaint brought to my attention by many a pet owner. And the reason I feel it happens all too often is because the training procedure is dismissed too soon with the assumption that the dog has the idea. There are some, but very few, puppies that can be trained in a couple of weeks. I never trust the puppy until it's six months or older. You have to be on top of this issue. After a few weeks, the biggest mistake people make is not taking the time to watch and make sure the dog has gone. Owners turn the job over to their kids or just assume the puppy has the idea of what to do. Big NO-NO! Constant monitoring must be the top priority for the first several months, and you can do this by giving the pup limited freedom in the house. The use of a kennel will make potty training a breeze. After a nap or a night's sleep in the kennel, always take your puppy to its potty place either outside or on the housebreaking pads and watch to witness it happen; if it doesn't, put that ball of fur in its kennel and try again in five minutes. This habit is the most important one to form. You don't want this sweet, cute four-legged family member to start going potty behind the couch or under the table, and believe me, your dog will find its own secret places to go.

Keep the puppy in a cleanable area, not on the carpet, until you're sure it has caught on to the idea. Use the same door and the same command each time you take it to go potty. Many people hang a bell on the door handle so that each time you go out you take the puppy's paw and ring the bell. Then proceed outside. Your puppy will catch onto this trick quickly. When you allow some freedom for your new pet, start by keeping all the other doors to the house closed (bathroom, bedroom) to slowly develop trust. There are certain breeds that tend to be harder to housebreak, which means you must be very confident with your training.

If you choose to use the housebreaking pads, great. I love this potty training method, especially for smaller breeds owned by elderly people and those of you living in apartments or condos. You will be able to put the pads anywhere you go, and the puppy can use them. It saves you and your dog from inclement weather like pouring rain or heavy snows. Dogs don't like to go outside and potty in that kind of weather anyway. Using pads doesn't mean your dog won't learn to go outside; most will go in both places. It simply gives them the ability to go potty on a designated area if you work long hours or can't make it home on time. The housebreaking pads are very clean and odorless, and they can even go into a litter pan if you like.

Whichever method you choose, stick with it faithfully and patiently, for we want this habit to be one that is truly ingrained in the training.

If you're adopting an older dog or found a stray, just pretend it is a puppy. You'll learn quickly if the dog is housebroken or needs training.

See - Kenneling

Private Parts - We all have them and so do our dogs. Keep them clean and free from urine build-up or stool cling-ons. Especially watch puppies because they don't wash themselves well. Use those wonderful baby wipes. Obsessive licking of private parts should not be happening. This could be an indication of an anal gland problem, urinary tract infection, vaginitis, etc. Discharge from this area should be investigated unless you have a female in heat or ready to give birth or that has just given birth. Otherwise, seek your vet's assistance. Male dogs sometimes drip a greenish discharge, which can leave a stain on the floor or carpet. If it is excessive, bring it to the attention of your vet. Again, keeping the area clean by using the baby wipes may clear up this issue.

See - Urinary Tract Infections

Puppies - Who on this earth can resist a puppy? They're beautiful, full of innocence, love, and joy. We feel all this in ourselves when we hold one of them. They are great healers for us, whether you know it or not. They also are very fragile at this time of their lives and rely on us for protection. Remember, puppies are building their immune systems too, so start the immunizations with your vet. Until all puppy shots have been given, keep them safe from being around a lot of dogs or dog parks. I would hold them when you're at the vet's office, especially if they are tiny, since a number of dogs come and go through the clinic. Be very careful when excited children hold and walk with your puppy. It's best to have the children sit on the floor and play with it. Also, be faithful and dedicated to the training during the first year of its life. Read, take classes, and really make a bond with your newfound friend. Remember, the two of you have a long life together ahead of you. The first year may be the hardest. Never underestimate what a puppy can get into. Use your kennel when you can't watch your puppy for its safety and your sanity. And just like babies, a puppy needs time out to sleep and grow. Even if you work at home, form a pattern where the puppy is in its kennel during part of the day. This also helps with separation anxiety by letting the pup be alone and bond to its kennel. Most behaviors are formed due to our inability to discipline and form boundaries. You're not being unloving or cold but creating a loving and acceptable living partner in your home. Hold true to the training needed to form a wonderful companion that will spend many years living with you.

See – Anxiety, Kenneling, and Potty Training

Quake
Quarantine
Queasy
Quills

*"Quiet" - the appreciation for others
to enjoy their serenity.*

Quake - Quaking, shaking, or trembling happens if your dog is in fear mode. The best antidote for this is to not respond. When you try to console or comfort your pet, it will quake all the more. In the dog's mind, when you touch it during the quaking, it's a form of reward, so you magnify the behavior. If it's upset or frightened, place it in its kennel, its safe spot. Cover the kennel with a sheet, and play a radio. Use this routine, and you'll soon see your dog go in on its own for the security. After all, you don't want your bed vibrating during a storm.

See – Anxiety, Fireworks, and Thunder

Quarantine - It means to keep your dog away from other pets if you suspect it has a sickness that can spread to other animals. Kennel cough, sneezing, and vomiting are some indications that you should consider quarantining your dog. Have a place and a set of bowls separated for this dog, if other dogs are in the household, until you get an okay from the vet or the symptoms subside.

Queasy - *See Motion Sickness*

Quills - Where I come from, many a dog has encountered

quills in its face. If you travel or hunt in porcupine country, make sure you read up on how to get quills out. Many times the dog must see a vet immediately to be anesthetized for quill removal. Carry a pair of pliers in your pack, and, I have heard, if you cut the quill it will release air, which makes removal easier. Fido ain't gonna like it much either. If your dog gets the quills in its mouth or throat, a vet is needed immediately. Finding your dog in a panic state is stressful for all. Try to remain calm and get to some help. And don't think your dog has learned its lesson, if given the chance it will do it again.

Raccoons
Rawhides
Roached Back and Tail Down
Rock Eaters
Rolling In Sh_ _
Rubber Bands
Runaways

"Responsible" - having the wherewithal to be accountable to the needs of these great creatures, our dogs.

Raccoons - Cute, cute, cute. This masked little varmint is all over the U.S. raising havoc and spreading illnesses to many of our domestic four-legged friends, which also can affect you in some cases. Their urine is very hazardous to our dogs and us, so don't encourage them to stay around your yard. Feed birds away from dog areas to avoid raccoons coming in the yard for the bird seed. Even with regular vaccinations, your dog may not be protected in some situations. If you notice a loss in appetite, sluggishness, or lethargy with some vomiting involved, have your vet check for leptospirosis, which can be transmitted to you or your dog through urine. This illness attacks the kidneys, so don't waste any time in getting to your vet. Also, remember that these cute little bandits will attack your dog too, so always check your yards before an evening potty break.

Rawhides - What a market this is. Most dogs love them, and they come in all flavors and coatings, which when chewed on can gum up and stain your carpet—what fun. Rawhides are a great dog sitter, a way to occupy its time. However, too much of anything isn't good. Some dogs just won't stop chewing them until they're gone, then at one a.m. you hear the familiar gagging and glugging sound. Know your dog and how it eats rawhides. Buy larger ones so no choking can occur, and throw them out when they become a swallowing hazard. And by all means, limit how many are given. Ask your vet because they can become a problem with the digestive system if too many are eaten.

See - Throat

Roached Back and Tail Down - This is an indication of a back injury.

See - Back and Hunched Back

Rock Eaters - That's right—some of our four-legged friends love rocks. Some develop intense rock fetishes with a constant focus on any rock, causing anxiety and crazy nonstop searching for rocks. Breeds such as Retriever types and Newfoundlands have a tendency to pick up any item and prance it around in proud display, and this can include rocks of all sizes. As the owner, you must take on the role of rock police. This habit starts when the dog is young, digging up rocks, retrieving rocks thrown in shallow water, and so on. Sooner or later one goes down the hatch and will need to be removed surgically. That solves one rock dilemma; however, the rock fetish still exists. Discouraging all picking up, playing, and digging of rocks at a young age is the first order of business. Taking the dog away from the area breaks the focus on the rock or whatever they shouldn't have. Being vigilant over your pet when it is in the yard can and will stop this habit. Again, it's up to YOU!

See – Savings Account

Rolling in sh-- - Dogs love to do this. They find it and dive right in, mashing it on the sides of their neck and all over the collar. If you have ever watched a dog perform this ritual, it's hard to imagine why it would roll in sh_ _! And, of course, the dog does it right before you leave for work or take it into the car with you. Usually, this aromatic debris is from a raccoon, possum, or deer. And it doesn't stop at sh_ _. It could be a dead frog, bird, deer carcass, fish, whatever. A dog just can't help itself. One theory is that the dog does this to disguise itself, cover up its scent like in the days of its ancestors. And my advice is . . . it's going to happen—they're dogs. Just get a pail of warm water and wash them off. It's part of being a dog owner. You could watch your dog's every move in the yard, but then you wouldn't have a story to tell your friends. We need that sort of drama so we have a story to tell at work.

See – Bathe and Shampoo

Rubber bands - I bring this subject up because of an experience I once was told about. Please tell your kids to never put any type of rubber band on the dog, ever. Kids don't realize how devastating and painful this event could end up being. And kids don't mean to harm the dog. The incident I knew of was done in playful fun, but the rubber band was forgotten, causing the dog to lose its tail a few days later. So please spread the word.

Runaways - Owning a dog that is a runaway (as I do) does take some of the fun out of dog ownership. It's an extra worry to always be on guard because it only takes one time for the running away to be fatal. It is a frustrating trait in a dog and one that isn't easily broken. I find that a dog that runs is fixed in the moment and is so intent with the sense of freedom or fear that it doesn't know where to go next. There is absolutely no focus on anything; it runs hither and yon searching for who knows what. The dog also doesn't have a clue about cars or any danger to itself. Then, of course, you start chasing, creating a game in its mind. You panic, scream, and yell its name, and don't forget the cursing. I'm really good at that, and around it goes. So in this runaway journey, many of us must endure. I have some advice on how to control the situation, which I am happy to share with you.

1. Never let the dog go to the door. Train it to sit back from the door with a command and hand signal until you say "come." This can be practiced on every door in the house and is very easy to teach. I reward the dog with love and sometimes a treat.

2. Leave a leash on the dog during the training period. It gives you grabbing ability if the dog should get out.

3. Make sure that the pooch can't slip out of the collar. Dogs can become Houdini with the collar trick. I like the martingale collar; it's a cross between a choke and regular collar. Dogs can't slip out of this one.

4. Make sure you have an ID tag attached to the collar.

5. Always carry a special treat in your pocket. It could be all you need to lure your dog over, especially if it is a food-monger.

6. Try not to chase Fido. In our panic, it's instinctive to chase and try to catch it, but it

rarely works. The dog will only run faster.

7. This is a hard one for me, but always reward the dog when you catch it. A wooden spoon comes to mind, but a dog remembers your negative reaction and may not come next time.

These types of dogs will slow down with age, but, I for one will never fully trust them. A fenced yard will help your peace of mind and your dog's life. Many dogs in fenced yards can become escape artists, so make sure to plug any holes in the fence and keep it tight to the ground. If your dog runs for a sense of adventure and not fear, a way to get it to return is to use a "calling" device that has a squealing sound, like that coming from an injured rabbit or squirrel. There are turkey calls or rabbit calls at your local hunting stores that can get your dog's attention. Get on the ground with your back to the dog and start the animal squealing. Your dog wants to hone in on that injured animal, so when it gets close try to grab it. From deep down in that blood-pressure-filled body of yours, praise the dog for coming to you. Believe me, the squealing noisemaker really works. Remember to not make a game of it in the house; save it for seek and recovery missions only. Those that run out of fear are much harder to catch. Sometimes they will get in the car if you can get close enough to them. Finding a remedy for a fear runner is tough. If your house is active due to kids and friends, leave a leash attached to the collar for something to grab on to. A professional trainer is always advised, along with the super dog training programs that are on Animal Planet and National Geographic. Again, you must do the training actively to get the results you're looking for.

See – Fencing, Harness, Identification Tags, and Leashes

S

"Success" - focusing your commitment on a task until the results you have practiced are performed with ease.

Savings Account - It's just that, a savings account with your dog's name on it. It's a weekly tithing to your pet in times of need. Use a coffee can if you wish, but just start one. The peace of mind knowing you have money ready and waiting when needed is a restful feeling. Every year there are visits to the doctor and medications to purchase. This eliminates any money stress when those visits take place. In a situation where a costly treatment is required, you don't have to even think about the money because you have been saving. I hope you try it.

See - Insurance and Money

Scratching - *Ch'ing, ch'ing, ch'ing* is the sound that drives you crazy when the dog tags are flailing every which way and your dog is intensely digging its body over and over again. There is moderate scratching, which is normal, and then there is severe scratching. Radical scratching is definitely a sign to you that your dog has a problem. Pay attention; check its body for the reason behind the scratching. Fleas, allergies, welts, hot spots, and infected ears all cause awful scratching. Flea treatments are very helpful to control flea infestations on the dog's body. However, if this tiny pain-in-the-butt bug bites a dog that is allergic to the flea, you're going to have scratching even if you treated your pet. Talk to your vet about the best flea control for the particular area in which you live and be very diligent about repeating the treatment every thirty days. Some dogs are just allergy prone and have a heck of a time scratching their life away. There are many new foods on the market to help with scratching, along with antihistamines you can get from your vet that will calm down your poor dog's skin. Remember, dogs don't know when to quit, so you have to help them with:

1. Understanding the source of the scratch;
2. Giving soothing baths with oatmeal or medicated shampoos;
3. Ask your vet about antihistamines;
4. Treat for fleas;
5. Use a cone if needed;
6. Apply anti-itch cream, such as cortisone or Caladryl, to the irritated area; and
7. Cover with a t-shirt to protect affected area.

If these suggestions do not help, a trip to the vet will be next on your list. Many times a little treatment with a drug called prednisone is in order to give relief to the craziness. When this is prescribed, be aware that your dog's thirst and hunger will increase. This means more trips outside.

See - Allergies, Fleas, Food, Hot Spots, Mange, Staph Infection, and Yeast Infections

Seasonal Allergies - Scratching, sneezing, biting of the feet and body, and red inflamed ears and skin, can all be symptoms of seasonal allergies. They usually start in the spring when the grasses begin to grow and the buds on the trees begin to pop. Another bothersome time of the year is around August 15th right through November. Always check and treat for fleas during this time of the year. Seasonal allergies should be treated with Benadryl or something from your vet to soothe the skin. Baths with an oatmeal or anti-itch shampoo along with a baking soda rinse can give some relief to our itchy friends.

See - Allergies

Seizures – Glazed-over eyes, clenched mouth, foaming or drooling, stiff body, shaking or quivering, loss of bowels or urination, inability to stand—these are symptoms of a seizure. Some last sixty seconds and others thirty minutes. There is no need for panic or racing to the vet during the episode; it usually is over before you're in the car. Your dog will be a little unstable for a while, but then it will go back to normal behavior. Mini-seizures most commonly appear around two years of age in some pets, while others never have an episode until the senior years. Epilepsy is generally the cause in the two-year-old pets; however there are many reasons for seizures: stress or aging health, just to name a couple.

Having one seizure and not another for a long period of time is common with many dogs. Repetitive or frequent seizures definitely need the attention of your vet. Be sure to record these episodes on a calendar so you can track a pattern. There are wonderful drugs to control the seizures, and it's relatively inexpensive. So, if you witness your dog behaving as described above, just be calm and help it through the episode. You can talk to the doctor about it when the next visit occurs.

Self-feeding - Self-feeding is a method of feeding your dog that many owners love. It entails putting some food in a bowl and leaving it down until your pet eats it and then refilling the bowl. Simple! No morning or evening fuss or muss. Many dogs do very well as grazers by not overeating and maintaining a great body weight for many years. However, if you are noticing some girth around the mid section, the only way to totally control body weight is by measuring an exact amount of food and adding or subtracting a little at a time. By this I mean no more self-feeding. The bowl must be taken up, and meals must begin. The manor in which this is accomplished is by measuring what you would normally put in the bowl and decrease by one-third, which will be divided into two meals offered in the a.m. for ten minutes and in the p.m. for ten minutes. If the dog doesn't eat, do not offer the meal again until the next scheduled feeding. This will be a real test to see how strong you can be without caving in to those eyes. If not much weight is lost in a few weeks you will have to dial down one-quarter more each time until the right amount has been measured. You can't expect an overweight dog to self-feed and lose weight. This same idea can be used on a dog that seems disinterested in eating. The reason is your pooch gets bored with the food sitting there all the time. Offering a meal at a specified time starts them dancing and begging for a dinner. All I ask is that you try this suggestion for one week. If it isn't your thing, then just go back to your old ways.

See - Diet, Obesity, Overeating, and
Stubborn Eaters

Senility - Many senior canines experience senility. It might seem like your dog has almost gone back to puppyhood, requiring you to be watchful. Potty accidents, loss of eyesight and hearing, puppy-like behavior, and confusion about its surroundings all play a part. Put a bell on your pet so as not to lose it. Go back to kenneling if needed, and never let the dog out without supervision. This is just part of the geriatric era. There are some medications to try if you wish.

See – Aging, Doggy Diapers, and Kenneling

Seniors - Stately, wise, respected, hearty, and seasoned describes many dogs that become seniors. White-faced, bow-legged, fragile, and senile are also descriptions of our senior friends that we have become attached to. Our seniors are very special, and their dedication to us through their years of life is astounding. Having steadfast loyalty to us through all the lumps and bumps life offers without one complaint on how they are sometimes ignored. They are the best example of unconditional love that we have in this world of ours. It is our duty to provide them, as they age, with the comforts of a soft bed for their joints, a senior diet for an aging digestive system, guidance for the aging eyes, attentive to the loss of hearing, tolerance for the potty accidents, forgiveness for the aromatic breath in our faces, acceptance for wobbly old legs trying to climb stairs, and in the end the powerful decision to let go. Owning a dog is a fabulous partnership. One of devotion, responsibility, patience, true joy, and, at some point, loss. All of these are part of life's transitions, and my hope for you is the everlasting memory filled with love and laughter that we feel for our dog or dogs who share life's journey with ours. Senior dogs will encounter health issues, so be prepared and use the savings account. Rely on your instincts and your gut when enough is enough. Always view the situation from a quality of life standard for both you and your pet.

See – Aging, Euthanasia, Hearing Loss, Incontinence, Kenneling, Pad Wax, and Senility

Shade - Please be aware that your dog needs shade in the summer. Move the doghouse to a shady area or conjure up some type of sun block for it. The change in temperature from sun to shade is enormous, so please pay attention. The use of plastic tarps tied to the side and top of an outdoor kennel will give enormous relief from the blazin' sun.

See - Doghouses and Heat Exhaustion

Shampoo - This subject can be a huge, mind-boggling discussion if you go into a large pet store and look at all there is to choose from. All kinds of shampoo for every kind of dog, type of hair, or type of skin (shampoos to whiten or darken, types for sensitive skin, dermatitis, no tears, wonderful fragrances, or other treatments). Which one do you chose? I'll try to direct you. If you have a good ole fashion hearty dog, big or little, with no skin issues, you can use anything your heart desires, even if it is people shampoo. Just be sure to rinse all the shampoo out of the hair. Now, if you have an allergy sensitive dog, you'll want to use an oatmeal type or all-natural, soap-free shampoo, possibly one your vet suggests. There are many of these types of shampoos in pet stores. If you have a dog with dermatitis and lots of dead skin or dander, try some people dandruff shampoo and let it set for five to ten minutes before rinsing. You should shampoo weekly for dermatitis.

If it's fragrance you're looking for, nothing beats Lambert Kay Fresh and Clean shampoo and conditioner. This product's aroma will linger on, especially if you use it weekly. When your dog walks past you and you smell the shampoo in the air, that's award-winning product.

Your vet has many different types of shampoos for skin issues, so he or she may send you home with one that works best for a specific reason.

If you have a white dog and want to keep it white, well, there's a shampoo that's right up your alley. Lambert Kay makes Snowy Coat or Diamond Blue by Cardinal Laboratories, Inc., and Double K's Alpha White is another good whitening shampoo. Be sure to use it weekly, and you'll be wearing sunglasses to look at your dog. It really will whiten the hair right up.

If you have a shampoo that seems so thick it's hard to spread, don't be afraid to dilute it with some water so the consistency is easier to lather on the body. It will treat the skin and hair, and is just as beneficial but much easier to rinse.

Most of us live with these beasts in our homes, so get familiar with the shampoo of choice, as well as how and when to use it.

See – Bathe, Grooming, and Hair

Shedding Dogs- We all have our favorite breed of dog we are comfortable living with. Some shed very little while others leave hair everywhere. There's fur that collects and it's self-rolling across the wood floor, and there is the needle hair that likes to weave itself into the furniture, making for hours of vacuuming. Both types are keeping the sticky roller companies rich. I have a remedy that I have talked many a Beagle, Pug, Labrador, Retriever, Collie, German Shepherd, and assorted like mixed pooches into, and that is to get a haircut. Most at first were hesitant, but once they tried it, they loved it. I cut all those with needle hair using a #7F blade in the winter, and a #10 blade in the summer. For the dogs with roll-around hair, I use a #4F blade for a little longer cut, or right down to a #7F blade for that summer sleek Speedo look. Shedding is a big complaint with most dog owners, so I urge you to try it just once. I know I'll get you hooked.

See - Grooming and Hair

Shop Vac - Every home needs one of these contraptions, whether you have a pet or not. I'm talking a one-gallon shop vac used strictly for cleaning up wet messes. If you have a young or old dog that has potty accidents, this wonderful machine will do the trick. It's fantastic for yellow vomit, urine, and don't forget diarrhea on that white carpet. It's got you covered.

Here's how to use it. The vac comes with paper filters and a foam filter. Throw them out—they aren't necessary. Attach the hose and snap it together. Now you're in business. Mix up some soapy water in a container (you can use your laundry detergent, but very diluted). Then in another container mix up diluted liquid fabric softener. You'll also need plain tap water. Take all of these along with your shop vac to the designated area. Plug in the vac and suck out as much of the mess as you can first. Then pour the soap on the area, scrub, and suck it out, twice. After that, pour the softener down, rub it around, and suck it out. Lastly, rinse with plain water. If it's a stool mess, I advise you to pick up a majority of it and flush it down the toilet before you begin cleaning.

Always empty the shop vac and allow it to completely dry before storing, or it will rust the parts. Ta-dah, you're done—no stain and no smell. You're welcome.

See - Poop, Soft Stool, Urine, and Vomit

Skunk Spray - I've heard of many concoctions, but not one beats the other. Time, time, and more time is the best solution. The odor gets better every day, but you will smell it for a full year whenever your dog gets wet or damp. I do urge anyone who lives in a skunk-ridden area to always have the preferred product on hand. Usually, this is an early morning or evening event. Dogs that have just been sprayed will spread that smell all over your home with intense magnitude. Keep your dog outside if it has been sprayed by a skunk until you have applied the preferred product. Open all windows and doors and put fans in them or in the doorway to suck the odor out of your home. Also remember to use old towels when washing your pet because they will be ruined. Skunks have become a big problem for people in the city. They have taken up living under sheds and decks. If you have a skunk family living near your home, call a professional to trap the skunk humanely and remove it from your yard. If you think your dog has learned its lesson, guess again. Try to check your yard before a nighttime or early morning potty break to save you an unwanted chore. My best advice would be to put your dog on a leash during high skunk times to prevent this, but for some reason people must like the hullabaloo rather than a simple temporary leash detail.

Smelly Dog - All dogs have an odor and so do we. But if a really strong smell is coming from the pooch, check its ears for an infection, check for stools caught on the back end, and don't forget about checking the neck area for the scented debris of a dead animal or dung that your dog rolled in. Infected ears are very smelly, and you'll need to see your vet. Also, dogs with the heavy fold on the lower jaw just behind the long canine tooth can get an infection in that fold which smells terribly, similar to fish. Be sure to check this area for soreness and red irritation.
If this is the case, clean the area, place Neosporin in the folds, and see your vet for antibiotics. The rest just requires a good ole fashioned bath.
See – Bathe, Ears, Rolling In Sh--,
Shampoo, Sour Smell, and Swimming

Sneezing - Sneezing a little here and there due to seasonal pollen is very common. Radical, non-stop sneezing or daily bouts could be a sign of a medical issue coming on the horizon, so be sure to bring this to your vet's attention.
See- Allergies and Backward Sneeze

Snow - We in the North can relate to this white fluffy stuff. How fun it is to play in the snow, and our four-legged friends love it too. They love to bathe in it, dig and burrow their noses in it, chew and eat it, and chase snowballs. It's all great fun, but when the temperature goes sub-zero, take precautions. Below-zero temps can be dangerous for a dog, or any animal for that matter. They'll go out and in minutes be picking up one foot then another due to the frigid snow. Be sure to pack doghouses full of straw and check them daily during the sub-zero weather. Check your water source and food too. House dogs shouldn't be left outside long or walked for a very long distance until the cold weather breaks. Frostbite to the feet and ears are possible, so pay attention. Boots are available at pet stores or through catalogs but require some practice with wearing them. Entire outfits for winter are quite a market commodity nowadays, so you have no excuses for not protecting that pet of yours during inclement weather. There also is pet-safe salt available for steps and sidewalks at most stores.

Be sure to clear a path in your yard with a snow blower or shovel for all those itsy bitsy dogs that can be consumed by the snow. You'll find they really enjoy these paths and you can even make a maze for them to run around in for exercise. Back injuries can occur when the short, squatty ones have to jump through the snow to find a place to go potty. Let's not forget the balls of snow that attach to the legs and feet of the furry ones. It's so fun to walk in wet spot after wet spot as the snow melts, or have to give a warm water rinse to get the snow off. That sounds like another job for you. Why not try keeping the legs, feet, and belly area cut short? This will help tremendously while leaving body hair for warmth. Do what you want—but I personally prefer my socks dry.

Soft Stool - This is bad news in the house for sure and has shop vac written all over it. Many things can cause soft stool: viruses, your dog got into something, health issues, and let's not forget a food change. But the bottom line is, if it doesn't stop in a day or two, go to your vet. Never wait with a young dog because it is easily prone to contracting serious illnesses due to a lack of vaccinations.

When you are aware of an abnormal stool, always start the recipe in the *Diet* category with an organic, plain yogurt and Imodium for two to three days. (Always check with your vet on the amount of Imodium to give to your dog depending on its size). If the problem persists, see your vet. Stools can change with a senior dog too. Its body has a hard time digesting fats, so do get on track by asking your vet about a diet change.

Parasites or worms are another cause of soft stool. Having the stool tested at your clinic will solve this mystery. And with the proper meds it will clear up right away.

Throughout the year there also are viruses that rear their ugly faces. Vomiting, diarrhea, and lethargy are good indicators of this plight. A quick trip to you know who will start the healing process immediately.

Nervousness can produce soft stools in a matter of a couple of hours, so be aware and prepared if your dog tends to react in this manner when anxious.

Soft stool can collect easily around the rectum of dogs with long hair. Keeping this area clean is of utmost importance to prevent a stool blockage, along with a very raw and sore behind. Get help if needed to cut the hair away from this area. All groomers and animal clinics are very willing to aid you and your pet when this incident develops. Words to the wise: when noticing any sign of a soft stool, always keep your dog in a cleanable area until the coast is clear.

See - Diet, Giardia, Poop, Shop Vac,
Worms, and Yogurt

Sour Smell - A sour smell around your dog's head can be caused by a couple of things. Yellow vomit is one very sour odor that smells, even when dry, for many days. This pungent aroma attaches to the hair around the mouth or the hair on the ears and permeates your surroundings until you wash it off. Also, dogs that swim a lot in the hot and humid months develop bacteria around the neck and ears, which cannot be seen by the naked eye but definitely can be smelled by the human nose. You may be able to see a brown blotching on the skin on light-colored dogs. Use an antibacterial shampoo once a week following the instructions on the label for the duration of the swimming season, along with a good short haircut so the body can dry. Blowing them dry at the end of the day with the exhaust end of a shop vac or an air compressor with a blowing adaptor can really make a difference. Another big reason for a strong sour smell is runny eyes on dogs with folds on the sides of the nose. Keeping the hair short in this area and cleaning it daily can help, but the surefire way to eliminate this wetness is the use of Angel Eyes. If this doesn't do the trick, talk to your vet about getting a prescription for tetracycline. Even the dogs seem much happier with a dry nose.

See - Eyes, Smelly Dog, Stained Eyes, and
Swimming

Spaying - If you're a first-time dog owner, this subject is all about stopping the reproductive system of your female dog.

I'm all for it and promote it for all family pets. Not only is it healthier for the dog, but it helps to control unwanted litters of puppies. Just take a stroll through your local animal control or humane society, and then you may understand. Spaying your young female also aids in the avoidance of breast cancer and uterine infections, not to mention the bloody mess around the house for three weeks, which causes all the surrounding male dog population to hang around in wait of a possible fling with your little girl. Many vets perform spaying very early to eliminate possible pregnancy, which I support. But if you have a toy breed, for example a toy poodle, Shitzu, Maltese, Yorkie, etc., chances are many of the baby teeth won't fall out at five and a half months, which causes the adult teeth to come in right beside them.

These baby teeth need to be taken out and there's no better time than when you spay your little sweetie. I recommend having your dog spayed at six and a half to seven months, after all the adult teeth have come in. That way, any leftover puppy teeth can be extracted during surgery. Be sure to discuss this with the animal clinic that will do the spaying. It will save you another expense of surgery for the tooth extraction. Toy breeds have trouble with a shortage of room in their mouths for teeth, so the double teeth left in the mouth create decay sooner than you want. Large breeds rarely, if ever, have this happen, so they're safe to spay early due to the size of litters a large dog can deliver.

Please research this easy procedure and consider it.
See - Teeth

Springtime - Just a reminder that spring, with all its sounds and smells, has a tendency to promote ignorance and selective hearing in your pet, especially after being cooped up all winter. Beware of the neighborhood dogs if you're out walking, and carry your pepper spray to protect both you and your dog. Try to discourage your dog from drinking pools of water that formed from the winter thaw, as they are usually full of bacteria. This can cause a sick pup, vomiting, and the big D. Shop vac time. Make sure your ID tags are on your pet for fast return should it wander off in chase of the elusive squirrel.

See – Harness and Identification Tags

Stainless Steel Bowls - If you're in search of the best bowls for sanitation, nothing beats stainless steel. I'm pretty certain they even beat glazed crockery. The stainless steel prevents face pimples too.

See – Acne and Pimples

Staph Infection - If you are petting or scratching your dog, and you see or feel bumps, crusting, or pimple-like sores under the hair or on the belly, and it's digging or licking at the spot, you're probably dealing with a staph infection. Certain breeds get this infection more frequently than others, and age sometimes plays a big role. Don't panic: you won't catch it, nor will other pets in the house. Make an appointment with your pooch's doctor, and he/she will fix it up quickly. I do encourage the doctor visit because the infection will continue to spread, driving you and your dog crazy. This is very common during allergy season and can reoccur as your dog ages. Cutting the hair very short and using medicated shampoo can be helpful. With treatment, you will see great results in two days, giving your poor dog some relief.

See – Allergies, Itch, Pimples, Scratching, and Shampoo

Sticky Stuff - Gum, pine tar, or anything sticky can be removed with lighter fluid or Goo Gone. Put some on the sticky area and pick off the gunk. Then wash the hair with soapy warm water. Usually, the substance is on the hair anyway. Don't be afraid; these products won't burn the dog's skin because you're using only a small amount and washing it off immediately.

Stinky Ears - *See Ears and Sour Smell*

Stinky Mouth – Pe-ew! Good luck if you get stuck in your car with a dog that has a stinky mouth. Bad teeth and gingivitis are a big reason for this problem. Keeping your dog's teeth and gums clean is vital. Read about teeth and you'll learn how. Another reason for a very strong smell from the mouth can be the floppy skin with many folds that some dogs have. I see this often with Cockers and Springer Spaniels. The main fold on the lower jaw becomes raw with a very red or sometimes greenish color and a rotten smell of dead fish. It is a very tender area and will need to be cleaned with peroxide and use of triple antibiotic cream until you see your veterinarian. I've seen it clear up with an antibiotic treatment. You'll want to treat this problem or you may be driven out of your own home.

See - Bad Breath, Smelly Dog, and Teeth

Stomach Acid - Many dogs have an overabundance of acid, as we do, and leave ever-so-wonderful piles of yellow deposits on your freshly cleaned carpet or bed linens. This can be daily or a few times per week. Many doctors will prescribe antacids such as Pepcid in the a.m. and p.m., and tell you to be sure your dog gets some food at least twice daily. Even a piece of toast, as the food helps with absorption of the stomach acid. If you have an older dog, vomiting can be caused by food that's too rich or can be an indication of a health problem, so talk to your vet about this as well as food that would be suitable for your dog's age.

See – Bile, Gastric Acid, Shop Vac, and Stomach Acid

Stool Blockage - Many owners of new fluffy puppies or dogs with long hair must pay close attention to the hair that grows around the rectum. Keeping this hair cut away from the rectum so the stool can drop off freely and not get stuck is very important. Trimming their rear end not only helps them but will keep your carpet clean. If a piece of stool gets hung up on the hair, your dog will scoot on your wonderful carpet in an effort to remove it. And that ain't pretty! Your groomer or animal clinic will be glad to assist you with this ever-so-important beauty treatment.

See - Cling-ons, Poop, and Soft Stool

Stubborn Eaters - I certainly don't have this problem. Lots of dogs are just not big eaters. They'll turn their nose up at many offerings of food while the owners are worrying and fussing, trying to conjure up all kinds of entrées, only to have FiFi turn and walk away. I will admit, this type of hound will cause you to worry and buy and try all kinds of food.

A stubborn eater is just that, and you must stop pouring your attention into it. Your pet won't starve itself. We humans have such a love affair with eating that we push and push food, wanting everyone and everything to eat the way we do. Most of the time, the owner has caused this stubbornness to magnify by offering so many different menus that the dog will wait it out to see what the next entrée will be. Try offering the food twice a day for five minutes. If your dog refuses the food, take it up until the next meal. If it's hard food you're using, soak it in hot water for a few minutes to create an aroma, and then drain the water off. If you will just get the hound's appetite going, I guarantee it will eat for you, and regularly too. What generally happens is the owner can't hold out, and then a pattern begins. We need to watch older dogs for possible health problems that can cause them to lose their appetites. Your doctor can aid with this sometimes through medication that stimulates the appetite. Cooking up a diet your dog likes may be your answer rather than feeding dog food, and it's very simple and inexpensive to make. You can cook up a month's worth of food and freeze it in individual cartons, thawing one each day, if you like. Many different recipes on the internet also are available to choose from. Certain people also find cooking for their pet is rewarding, while others have no time for it. You decide.

See - Diet and Self-Feeding

Stuffed Animals - What great fun these fluffy stuffed things are for many a dog. Chewing them, shaking the heck out of them, pulling, tug of war, and let's not forget falling in love with them too. Thrift stores have them for practically pennies on the dollar and all sizes, shapes, and colors. Ripping them apart and strewing stuffing all over the carpet is a great pastime for many. Chewing plastic eyes and noses off seems to be a given also. Try to pick up all plastic pieces to prevent vomiting later in the night, like on your bed at three a.m., if you know what I mean. And take away any toys that cause the dog to growl or behave in a possessive manner. These toys are for play, not for control. Stuffed animals are a wonderful helper with a new puppy you have just brought home. It gives the pup something to cuddle and snuggle up to and helps ease the transition of losing its litter mates.

Sucking on these stuffed creatures can be a common habit. The favorite toy provides a calming, nurturing effect for many dogs. So don't panic when you find your pet in a state of utter bliss while nursing the heck out of its stuffed baby. Just like children need their favorite blanket to relax, your pooch also enjoys contented moments with its soft companion.

Submissive Wetting - You come home from work and look, talk, or—heaven forbid—reach down and pet your dog, when what to your wondering eyes should appear but a puddle of urine! "Oh dear." This is a very common complaint, especially from new puppy owners. I've seen this occur in very shy dogs and very happy ones, but the good news is this can be stopped without too much effort. Here are a few pointers that may be of assistance in stopping submissive wetting. Everyone in the household, including guests, must partake in the process. When anyone enters the home, do not look at, talk to, or pet the dog for five to ten minutes. Totally ignore it. If you kennel the dog, wait five minutes to bring it out to potty, and still say nothing and do not make eye contact until it has completed its potty. Your dog will stop when you alter your method of communication with it, ending the frustration. Very few adult dogs will continue to wet when they have either calmed down or built confidence in themselves. However, puppies take a while.   The way you respond to the dog will either help to stifle the reaction or encourage it. It's best to have some paper towels and disinfectant ready until you have the responses down pat. With diligence and perseverance, you will conquer this behavior, and when you do, you'll probably start wetting yourself out of joy.

See – Obedience and Shop Vac

Sun - Dogs love the sun as much as we do, often following it from window to window, then flopping down to absorb all the rays they can. They are not immune to injury from the sun either, especially light-colored pooches. Overheating can also occur, so make sure there is shade available and lots of H_2O.

Sweat - Do dogs sweat? Have you ever found doggie deodorant in your local pet store? How about doggie do-rags for the brow? The answer is yes. They sweat through the pads of their feet and by breathing or panting to cool their bodies down. The body has no sweat glands at all, but there are some in their feet and ears. This is another reason to keep the mouth and teeth clean: for sweeter smelling dog breath. Help them out when they are hyperventilating by putting them in a cooler atmosphere.

See – Heat Exhaustion and Panting

Swimming - They either love it or hate it. You're either trying to keep them out because they've been swimming all day or you're trying to get them to wet their feet. For those dogs that love to swim, be sure to use an ear-drying solution at the end of the day to help with stinky ears. You can make up a bottle of one part alcohol to one part white vinegar; squirt it into both ears at the end of the swimming day. Dogs with big heavy ears and a lot of hair are at higher risk for ear problems because it takes a long time for the ears to dry out. When the ears are heavy, air has a hard time circulating in the ear canal. I suggest keeping the hair on the ears short, at least for the swimming months. The hairy wet ears can develop a very musty, moldy stench to them, and the skin can develop a fungus if it isn't allowed to dry out.

If you take your dog on a boat, consider purchasing a swimming vest. They are bright in color and in addition to helping a dog swim will make it visible to other boaters. Many water dogs such as Labs and Retrievers love to chase the waterfowl in our lakes. Please be aware that the big geese and swans can drown a dog easily, so pay attention when these fowl are present.
See- Ears, Fungus, and Sour Smell

Swimming Pool - What a great amenity and a treat for your family. Many dogs love pools as much as the owners do and sometimes use them more frequently than the owner. Dogs also escape the burden of adding the chemicals, checking the Ph levels, and forget about even vacuuming the wonderful thing. Sounds like a lot of work to me. Like kids, sometimes dogs get into the pool when no one knows, so keep a good eye on them. Young and old dogs are the ones to be more concerned with, so monitor them as well as teaching your kids too. Whoever is letting the dog outside should be sure to know the dangers of the pool. Teach your dog to use the pool's steps or provide an exit in case it should fall in without you knowing.

There are fabulous floating steps that attach to the lip of the pool to make for easy exit and save your liner too. Make sure the cover is on tight when closing the pool for the winter; this avoids your dog getting stuck underneath. Enough of this kind of talk. Enjoy the pool and be safe.

*"Trust" - the number one component
for successfully co-mingling in any relationship.*

Table Scraps - To give or not to give; that is the question?
I personally do not give table scraps for two reasons. The
first is: I found I had to use the shop vac for a couple of
days after table scraps, if you know what I mean. My dogs
could never tolerate the added goodies, and I get tired of
the messes. The second is: If you feed dog food plus table
scraps you have to watch out for weight gain. If you tend to
be a scrap feeder, the only advice I would give is to feed only
the foods that are not rich in fat. Meat grease or
chicken/turkey skin is an invitation to go straight to the vet
with a pancreas attack. Bread, potatoes, veggies, etc. are
okay. No gravy or shellfish either.

See- Fatty, Obesity, and Overeating

Tail – Oh, what a powerful signal of communication. These
tails are especially powerful if they have some length to
them. We can tell how our dog feels by just watching the
tail. If it's up and wagging, it usually means happy. If it's
down and between the legs, it shows nervousness or
submissive feelings or signs of a back injury. If it's straight
out and stiff, it's a good indication of focus towards
something. Stay watchful of this great mood indicator; it will
help you understand your dog better.

Remember, really long tails extend your dog's body, so if you live in a tiny house, you might want to consider a pooch with a stubby tail to save on space. Long tails show so much expression, but they can wipe out your end table decorations or a cup of hot coffee with just a turn of the body. There's all shapes and sizes, each one with a tail to tell.

Be watchful of excessive chewing of the tail. There are seasons during the year which can cause your dog to severely gnaw on its tail. Pay close attention and seek help from your veterinarian.

Talking To Your Dog - We all do it, and each and every one of us has a special animated voice that suddenly comes from our mouths. We only use this voice around animals and it is unique to each individual. The pitch and the pronunciation of the words and sentences are quite comical. And it isn't just the ladies either; I've witnessed big grown men falling into this category. By all means, talk your fool head off, for the more you do the healthier you are. The next time you interact with any animal, for that matter, just pay attention to the stress level in your body. There won't be any!!!

Tapeworm - This is a worm that develops from ingesting a flea, rodent, or dead wildlife. Telltale signs are rice-like segments around and on the hair surrounding the rectum. These segments break off the main tapeworm in the intestine and can also be seen in the stool. This parasite is easy to get rid of too; however, it is not covered in the heartworm medication as so many other parasites are. Your animal hospital can fix your dog right up with a pill for this worm or you can purchase one at any local pet store.

Carefully read the directions for dosage too. So during the summer months, keep an eye on the stool and the rear end.
See -Worms

Tear Stained Eyes - This is a complaint from all the owners with dogs that have light-colored hair. The tear stain causes quite a brown trail down the side of the nose, sometimes keeping this area very moist and sour smelling. There are two methods that I am aware of to control the staining. First, is the use of tetracycline for one month every day. Discuss this method with your vet. He/She may want to wait until your pet has been spayed or neutered and all the adult teeth are in before prescribing. Second, the use of a fairly new product on the market, Angel Eyes, is added to your dog's daily diet. Angel Eyes can be purchased in any pet store/catalog or amazon.com.
See – Eyes and Sour Smell

Teeth - And the magic number is ??? Twenty-eight teeth for puppies and forty-two for adult dogs. Puppy teeth will start to die and fall out around five and a half months old. Its breath will carry a very odd aroma until the adult teeth come in. Some toy breeds, i.e., Poodles, Yorkies, Chihuahuas, etc., have a tendency to hold on to some of the puppy teeth, causing double teeth to occur. These puppy teeth should be removed for good oral health. This is the one big reason I don't like to see toy dogs spayed or neutered before we know if all the baby teeth have fallen out. Please don't let your vet talk you into any sooner then six and a half to seven months for that type of surgery. Large breeds rarely if ever have this happen. Keeping your dog's teeth clean is very important, so learn to brush or wipe the teeth regularly. Make rubbing the gums and teeth a part of your routine to touch them and desensitize the fear of you fooling around in their mouth. Most dogs will start to build tartar around two years old. You can take your fingernail and scratch it off very easily. By five years and up, they may need a cleaning from their doctor to keep up with good oral hygiene. If you are faithful at brushing or wiping with a mixture of equal parts Listerine and water, this will help immensely with the bacteria that causes red, inflamed gums and mouth odor. Oxyfresh Oral Hygiene for pets is a fairly new product I have encountered. You simply add it to their water daily, and it eliminates bad breath as well as helps control tartar build up amazingly well. This product can be found at www.oxyfresh.com or 800-333-7374. I must testify it does work.

Pay attention to the whiteness of your dog's teeth to promote good health. There is a vaccine offered by some clinics to help control the bacteria in the mouth. It is fairly new, so there is not a lot of results back on how effective it is, but I have high hopes this is a great idea too.

Having your dog's teeth cleaned can be a shocking expense so again, I can't say enough about the savings account concept!

Don't be shocked if some have to be extracted. This is very common, and the dog does just fine if not better without the loose, rotten teeth in its mouth.

Abscesses often happen to older dogs and you'll know because their face will swell under the eyes or in this area. An open sore can even occur. There are antibiotics developed to focus on dental infections. Your vet will guide you with this decision.

Please try to brush, brush, brush and keep the pearly whites shiny and the breath sweet.

See - Bad Breath

Temperature - A dog's normal temp should be 101° to 102°. If your pooch is feeling a little out of sorts, it's very easy to take its temperature. When you're at the store, purchase a hand-held digital thermometer in the baby department, a cheap one costing six to ten dollars, and it should be kept in your First Aid Kit. Put some Vaseline on the end of it and gently insert it into the rectum until it beeps. It will immediately tell you the temperature and you will know if you should call your vet.

Thirst - *See Excessive Thirst*

Throat - Our dogs' throats really take a beating when you think about it. It's the part of the body where we usually attach these fancy, dancy collars or prong, choke, or shock collars to control our pets. We need to pay attention to the apparatus that we place around our dogs' necks. Make sure not to put them on too tight and also to change the size as they grow. My rule of thumb is three fingers should fit easily under the collar. There are wonderful harnesses that are designed to stop pulling (Gentle Lead) and those used to walk dogs or tie them outside to prevent the throat from getting choked. Pay attention to what your dog chews on and swallows. If a rawhide breaks down and becomes a dangerous size, get rid of it. Dogs can be like kids and get odd items stuck in the throat, so it's a good idea to pay attention.

Sharp meat bones and wood sticks should be taken away. The slivers from both of these items can stick in a dog's throat, causing irritation and possibly a visit to the vet.

Throats can also become raw and irritated during allergy season or an allergic reaction. The signal for this is the pooch wants to swallow constantly and is very anxious. They at times will even try to eat something bizarre, like your rug, to soothe themselves. If you can relate to this behavior, the best remedy I know of is to give a dose of Benadryl or a tablespoon of flavored brandy along with kenneling them to settle the situation down. Usually by morning the sensation has left and all is back to normal.
See – Collars, Harness, and Rawhides

Thunder - This sound can scare the bajesus out of many a dog, sending them high tailin' it to the hills, running anywhere to get away from the noise. Lots of pets come up missing during thunderstorms, and it seems they can hear it long before we do. Please keep an up-to-date ID on your pet if it is one that tends to run for its life out of terror. Pay attention if a storm is coming too, and put your dog in a safe place (kennel) if you will be away. One clap of thunder could cost you a sheet of drywall and molding, if you know what I mean. Tranquilizers are a benefit in calming an anxious dog, so talk with your vet. Spring is a fabulous season, except for that darn thunder.
See – Fireworks, Identification Tags, Kenneling, and Tranquilizer

Ticks - These creatures of nature can carry with them some mighty powerful diseases that can devastate your dog's health. Found commonly in lawns, bushes, tall grasses, and every state in the U.S., they are not to be taken lightly. Lyme Disease, Ehrlichiosis, Babesia, and Anaplasmosis are some of the transmittable illnesses that can manifest after a tick bite. When traveling to other states, be aware of the diseases common in that area. If a tick is found, remove it close to the body of the dog with some tweezers and take it to be analyzed at your veterinarian clinic. Another quick way to remove the whole tick is to apply enough liquid soap onto a cotton ball in order to cover the tick. In a matter of minutes, the tick will come right off, easy as pie.

Prevention is a must, especially if hunting and camping or hiking are part of your regular activities. Frontline for fleas and ticks is what is recommended, along with Frontline pump spray all over the body before an excursion in the great outdoors. There are wonderful facts online to keep you up to date and informed.

Toenail Snappers - These are pooches that just love to chew and snap at their toenails, especially when they are relaxing. Many dogs do this, so don't think yours is special. It's just a habit that they enjoy.

Toilet Water - The toilet bowl has been a watering trough for as long as I can remember. Large dogs love it because it offers such easy access to water. My only complaint is if they drink from the toilet, they should wipe the seat too. If your dog loves the toilet water, be sure not to hang those cleaners in the tank for safety. I should mention to flush often too.

Tolerance - The ability to be patient, to endure, to have a calm composure when your puppy is beginning its training. A one-day-at-a-time mindset, along with consistent teaching for many months, will ensure that not so far away in the future you will reap the thrill that it finally sank in.

Toothbrush - Absolutely!! I recommend the ones that rotate in a circular motion, but I'll settle for any type as long as you use it. Get your pet and yourself into the habit of brushing twice a week for gum and tooth hygiene. There is dog toothpaste available, but I prefer a mixture of equal parts Listerine and water to help with gingivitis.
See – Bad Breath and Teeth

Touch Training - This is a training command used in agility and service dog training; however, it is underused for home training. It involves a retractable pointer and some treats. Oh, and you'll need some training instructions too. There is information online about this method and also a successful trainer and her book called *Kathy Santo's Dog Sense*. I think you will find this a very fun and rewarding exercise to teach your dog with positive results.

Tranquilizers – There will be many situations in which your dog will need help to relax. Travel, thunder, and fireworks all create stressful feelings that can be relaxed with the use of a tranquilizer. If your dog becomes anxious to the point of running away or destroying doors as stress appears, talk to your doctor. He/she understands and can help provide relief to you and your pet with the right calming choice.

> *See - Anxiety, Fireworks, Kenneling, and
> Thunder*

Travel - Traveling with your dog can be a wonderful
experience, provided your dog is a good traveler. I advise
you to start acclimating your dog to travel from a young age;
however, even a newly adopted dog can become a great
traveling companion. Always keep your First Aid Kit, health
papers (vaccine records), identification tags, and an extra
leash with you wherever you go. Traveling in a vehicle can
become the home away from home when you get good at it,
and many hotels are very animal friendly all over the U.S. I
would recommend checking your route to pre-plan areas that
are pet friendly. Taking a kennel with you is always advisable,
especially for our tiny friends. But I think it's a must for all,
and here's why: your dog is always safe in a kennel; it can't fly
across the car or into the window or onto the floor if you
have to put the brakes on fast. It also is your dog's familiar
place, if you want to leave it at the hotel to sightsee or go
out and get a bite to eat. There are wonderful collapsible
cages on the market that don't take much space. I also love
the pet seatbelts that secure our dogs to one seat so they
can't be thrown across the vehicle, and it keeps them from
jumping all over the car, which can make a driver nervous. I
know we are all intelligent here, but I must mention one other
issue when traveling in the summer. Never leave your pet in a
hot car!!! If you are going to sightsee all day, find a boarding
kennel with air conditioning and go enjoy the day.

Teaching your dog not to be an excessive barker is
always high on my list. It's just plain courtesy to think of

people around in the other rooms or camp grounds. If you don't believe me, plan on packing up and hittin' the road, because you will be asked to leave if you can't keep your pooch quiet.

Now, let's talk a little on air travel. Of course the small ones can ride under the seat right along with you. But if you have never taken your pet before, I would suggest a little practice with the kennel and place it under your kitchen chair while you eat so it gets the idea of confinement before you go. This is also where I highly suggest a tranquilizer so your pooch can take a little nappy poo and relax through the air travel. Talk to your vet ahead of time and try the pill given before you go on your trip, because some tranquilizers do not work as well as others. I guarantee you that a restful dog is what you want. I would also plan my trip, if possible, to be nonstop, especially if you ship your dog in cargo. The ticket may cost more, so just save for it.

I can't comment too much about flying dogs in cargo except I know it is very common and large dogs must travel this way. Do your research and fly your pet with a pet-friendly air service. There are airlines that specialize in air travel for pets. Talk to them and, again, if at all possible, fly a nonstop flight. Feed a very light meal the night before and give them time in the morning or before you travel to empty their systems. Don't feed your dog the morning of air travel; it has enough body fat to miss a meal and this will prevent sickness. This also lessens its need for water during the trip. When you dog's voyage is for many hours, provide a nice thick absorbable bed in case of a potty accident. This way, it won't be laying in wetness. Many owners worry about their babies in travel, especially in cargo, but I can assure you, it's done everyday and with your dog's safety in mind. Please think positively in this situation. Relax knowing all is well and soon you'll be reunited with your pet to take off on the new adventure.

See – Motion Sickness, Vehicles, and Vaccines

Tylenol - DO NOT give this product to your dog! It is poisonous to your pet. Coated aspirin is available for pain relief. Check with the vet for the proper dosage.

"Unconditional" - the unequivocal devotion shown by our devoted furry friends.

Unconditional Love – This is a quality we should all aspire to harness. It seems natural to many animals on this planet, especially our domestic animals, to ooze positive energy. Do yourself a favor and pay attention to how your body feels when you interact or even watch animals, their babies, and our own young. Lock that emotion in your mind and practice the feeling of it in your everyday life. The use of unconditional love and laughter are proven to heal your body and certainly your soul. So please let your pets teach you a thing or two about living. You'll find this infectious.

Urinary Tract Infections - Many dogs experience this type of infection at some point in their lives and certain breeds are more likely to encounter this uncomfortable issue on a regular basis. Some indicators of urinary tract infections are: frequent and frantic need to go outside; when outside, going and going in many places; blood in the urine (don't panic: this is from straining); accidents in the house; anxiousness and panting with an inability to relax; and excessive licking of the private area. If you suspect a problem, try to catch some urine in a clean container. The first one in the morning is the best, and take the urine and your dog to the vet for a look-see. Usually antibiotics are given and your dog will feel relief in one day. Infections should not be common in your dog's life, and if they are, crystals and stones are more than likely lurking. Your doctor will perform some tests to confirm this. There are fabulous foods on the market today to control these painful infections and prevent stones from forming. Also, pay attention to the flow of the urine: it should flow and not trickle.

Another possible cause for a urinary tract infection is stress. Many dogs that are boarded get their systems so stressed that in a couple of days an infection takes hold. If your dog habitually comes home with an infection after being boarded, don't blame the kennel. Talk to your vet so you can have medication ready to give the caregiver before the problem gets severe. Nerves are the culprit in this case.

Some dogs aren't big drinkers, which doesn't help matters. I would recommend using distilled water and cover their food with it so they have to drink the water in order to get to the food. This might not look too appetizing, but it definitely helps, and they will get used to a soupy meal.

See - Bladder Stones, Diet, Distilled Water, and Frequent Urination

Urine (The Catching of the Urine) - This is a wonderful trick all dog owners should teach their dogs because at some point in your dog's life, it may be one of the most useful training methods. Urine catching is the ultimate game of trust between you and your dog. You teach your dog to urinate while you reach down and place a flat container under its you know what and catch the urine. Be sure the container is clean. This handy method is very useful if your dog has or you suspect is having a urinary tract infection or your vet needs to check the Ph levels for urinary balance. The best catch is the first urine in the morning, so hold off on the coffee till you catch the urine.

This procedure must be done in your pj's, underwear, or robe, so that your neighbors have something to talk about.

*"Vibration" - The invisible energy
that activates reaction by any living creature.*

Vaccines - I, for one, feel it is very important to vaccinate your dog. Your vet will set you up on a program if you have a puppy or a new adult dog. If you board your dog or have it groomed, make sure to get the vaccine for kennel cough, Bordetella. Many illnesses pass from dog to dog in the same manner as they do when school starts and kids get sick, so why not prevent issues from happening? If your dog is a runaway and ends up in doggy jail, your vaccines will save it from illness. Animal control picks up so many pets and puts them in these facilities that there's a high risk of contamination for any dog housed there, even for a few hours. When you retrieve your dog and take it home, you will infect any other pet in the house. So vaccinate! If you set up your savings account, you'll have plenty of money ready to pay for next year's prevention. Every state has its own rule on vaccinations and dog licensing, so make sure you know what's required whenever you move to a new state.

Traveling with your pet also requires vaccines and a health certificate, so be sure to do your homework when it comes time to taking your pet on an excursion.

See - Immunizations

Vehicles - I can get very long winded on this subject, so put the popcorn in the microwave and go potty, and then come on back and read this one. Who doesn't like to take their dog in the car, truck, van, motorcycle, or motor home with them? Most people love to haul their dogs everywhere they go. Some of you have adequate vehicles and some don't. Some buy a special car just to haul the dog, along with a special booster seat with seatbelts, water bowl, and maybe even headphones, if it'll wear them. Over the years, many dogs have come to my house in a vehicle driven by their own personal chauffer, and many different incidents have occurred, so I'm going to suggest some dos and don'ts to help you prevent issues in your vehicle.

Let's start with the <u>DOS</u>: <u>DO</u> take your dog with you whenever you want to. Be in charge and always invite your pooch, but don't let it assume that every time you go to the car it is going too. Be aware that most dogs love the car and being with you, so your dog may pitch a fit if it can't go at some point. It's important to teach your dog to be relaxed at home if you can't take it with you. I suggest using a kennel to protect your house from a disappointed dog. If you have a puppy or an adult dog that vomits on a car ride, carry paper towels and read up on how to use a shop vac. This doesn't have to be a life-long problem, but it will take a little bit of your time to help your dog overcome the anxiety. For a vomiting pet, take it every day or even several times a day on a short ride (five minutes at first). Ending up at a nearby park for a fun walk can become the reward, which makes the car ride a fun thing. You could even go around the block and follow that up with a walk, and with each week increase the time according to the saliva being produced (by the dog, not you). Very rarely will this not work. Some ride better in a kennel, some with a seatbelt. Whichever you choose, just be sure it's the safest for you, the driver, and your dog. Here's a big <u>DO</u> that you'll thank me for mentioning. <u>DO</u> take the keys out of the ignition when you put your dog in the vehicle. And wire a spare on the front of the car grill for when you forget and the dog steps on the lock button, locking you out. <u>DO</u> keep the windows rolled part way up. I can't tell you how many dogs jump out of the moving car after some object, and this can turn into a heartbreaking ordeal. If you like your dog to hang out the window, be sure it is hooked up to a seatbelt restraint so it can't jump out. <u>DO</u> have control of your pet while driving. You don't need them getting all tangled in your legs and the pedals for safety reasons. <u>DO</u> have your dog on a leash so if the car door is opened you can grab the leash.

Always have a spare leash in your car. If your vehicle breaks down, these wonderful leads make it safe and easy to walk or hold your dog while you figure out the next course of action.

These are some <u>DON'TS</u> that I hope will help you: <u>DON'T</u> leave your dog in a vehicle when the weather is hot. Sometimes even 70° can be too hot if the sun is beating down on the windows. Being in that hot car is like being in an oven, and it doesn't take long before your animal is very sick or worse. If you must travel with your pet in the heat and you need to stop, leave it in the car with the air conditioner running and have an extra set of keys with you when doing this. I would advise you to have your dog in a kennel or hooked up to the belt restraint, because some dogs love to stand by or on the power window buttons, and if you leave the car running with the air conditioner, all the automatic buttons are working. Thus, if the dog stands on the window button, guess what happens? Then you have a dog loose in the street. <u>DON'T</u> leave a young dog that loves to chew in your vehicle without being able to observe its behavior. It will destroy the steering wheel or seatbelt or anything that grabs its attention. When you order fast food and refasten your seatbelt, guess what scent is on the belt? Yum yum. Some dogs are chewers for a couple of years, so beware. <u>DON'T</u> transport your dog in the trunk of your car. If you don't want your dog on the seat, use a kennel or cover the seat with a sheet. <u>DON'T</u> ignore the power window buttons. If your dog is hanging out the window and steps on the up button, it can get itself rolled up and panic. Now, since it's standing on the button, you can't give immediate help, which causes you to panic while driving. So if you have a lock for the power windows, I would suggest using it. I've seen this happen, and it's very scary for you and your dog.

If you're a motorcycle buff and transport your pet in a trailer, please make sure to have the pooch belted in. Going at a fast rate of speed and hitting a bump can send your pooch sailing. Have fun!

See – Identification Tags, Kenneling,
Leashes, Motion Sickness, and Travel

Veterinarians - This is a very big deal. Find one you connect with, trust, and relate to. If you're new to the area, ask around and don't be afraid to change vets if you aren't satisfied with the one you've got. Get a second opinion if your dog has a major health problem or you feel you would like to investigate other options. You learn by asking questions along with doing your own homework.

I'm going to talk about cost now because that's what I hear comments about. Lots of pet owners get very upset with veterinary costs, and I will agree that I have witnessed some very hair-raising fees. I have seen many unfair charges issued to pet owners. However, I want you also to consider the cost of running a first-rate clinic, the cost of state-of-the-art equipment, staff's wages, and building expenses. You will, at some point during your dog's lifetime, have to ponder a major or semi-major issue, so start your savings account in preparation. You have time to save, and this takes the stress off the money worries, which allows you to focus on fixing your pet. There is no doubt that the cost of animal care is on the rise, so you must be prepared with a pet nest egg. If you live in a big city, they've got you captive, so check prices with different clinics. Your money is good anywhere, so you need to come up with your happy medium. Veterinarian medicine is growing with incredible medical procedures being performed in your local clinic. If you wish to treat your pet, which is totally your decision, cost is the name of the game. Diagnostic equipment is not cheap, and the cost trickles into the overhead of the clinic. There are clinics that offer more in-depth treatment or specialization, and then there are your basic animal clinics. It's up to you to decide what kind of veterinary clinic you need. Our pets become a big part of our family, giving back more joy, love, and laughter than you can put a price on. But for some odd reason, it is easier to pay a restaurant for an expensive meal that we flush the next day than it is to reimburse our vet for services that keep our pet healthy. Go figure!

See – Holistic Medicine, Insurance, Money, and Savings Account

Vinegar - Not the best smelling stuff, but it certainly can keep your dog's water bowl spic and span. Adding a tablespoon to four cups of water keeps it sparkling and prevents the mineral rings on the bowl. If your bowl is brown and dingy, pour white vinegar into it and within twenty minutes you can scrub it right back to new. This is your tip for the day.

Vodka - This is for you to take when the going gets rough. Get a glass, put in ice and a shot of vodka, some tonic and a lime. I guarantee within twenty minutes you'll view things differently and be a lot calmer. Now one is enough!

Vomiting - Come on now—we all know that guttural sound, that glugging over and over until, oh yes, that wad of grass or plastic toy piece or just plain yellow bile gets deposited on your carpet, bed, car, or even on you. Young dogs sometimes vomit several times in the course of a week because of what they ingest. Keeping toys and things picked up will really cut down on the mad race to the door. This event can be quite frequent for some dogs throughout their life. They form too much acid. Eating two to three times a day will help absorb the acid and in some cases your vet can suggest an antacid, which is helpful.

Many dogs are severely allergic to chicken products, which can be in the food you're feeding. There are other types of meat choices in dog food to relieve their stomach. Older dogs that start to vomit could be struggling with their diet also. Try a senior diet with 16-18% protein and speak with your vet about the food choice.

Vomiting should be controlled either with food change

or medication. If your dog seems out of sorts, it is important to discuss this issue with the doctor. Other times, dogs are just plain ole sick like we can get, and they may vomit six to eight times before stopping. They could have a virus or could have eaten something dead and spoiled. Your vet has medications to stop the vomiting and aid in their recuperation. Whatever event causes the vomiting, one thing is for sure: you'll need a shop vac and the dog will need a bath. At least wash the mouth and ear area if the hair is long, or you will smell it for days.

Monitor what your dog is chewing and take it away if vomiting occurs. Chewing is common in many dogs and can continue until age two or three. If possible, keep all bedroom doors closed until you notice less and less of this behavior. However, one breed comes to mind. The Airedale seems to chew and ingest for most of its life, so you'll never open those doors again unless you like cleaning up vomit.

Here are a few tips on vomiting:

1. Own a shop vac.

2. Ingested toy particles will be vomited and just make a mess, so take away toys that can be eaten and the vomiting will stop.

3. If the dog is throwing up several times every fifteen to thirty minutes, it probably has a bug. See your vet. If you are in a situation where you can't see the vet, here's what you can do in the meantime:

a. Pick up the water because they will want to drink, causing even more vomit. Give them ice chips, or better yet, Pedialyte squirted into the mouth;

b. Be calm; they may vomit just like us all night long at times. Keep them in a cleanable room or in a cage that you can clean; and

c. Give them Dramamine to dry up the mouth and stop the nausea. One pill for smaller breeds and two pills for medium and larger breeds is sufficient.

If you can't get medical help by the next day, don't feed them a lot at one time and use a bland diet for a few days. Most importantly, keep up on the Pedialyte or an electrolyte powder mixed into their water. Offer this several times to hydrate them. If the dog is not drinking, use a needleless syringe or dropper and squirt the electrolyte liquid into its mouth every ten to fifteen minutes.

If you have a very young dog that is vomiting and has diarrhea, get to your vet immediately. Even dogs that have had vaccines can still develop Parvo, which can be deadly and highly contagious.

Dogs are just like kids, they get sick and recover, so don't panic. Just always be prepared with your First Aid Kit. Keeping them isolated from other pets is important to control the spread of any illness.

See – Bathe, Bile, Diet, Gastric Acid, Lethargy, Pedialyte, Queasy, and Shop Vac

*"Worry-Free" - the state of being
we enjoy when the training is complete*

Walking - If you are an avid walker of your dog, you probably have to spell the word at times so that these four-legged crazies don't get all riled up. What a wonderful act of bonding this can be. Very few dogs dislike walking. It's a fantastic experience for both involved, providing a blend of exercise, interaction, and outside exposure of sights, sounds, and smells. While walking, remember you are the alpha dog; a walk is a walk, not a pee-fest or a pulling/sparring contest with other walkers and canine friends. Don't allow urinating on every post, pole, or fire hydrant. This habit is uncalled for. A walk means a walk, so let them relieve themselves first, than get on with the planned event. The proper collar or harness should be used when walking. There are many harnesses with special attachments for hooking on the lead to help with pulling and control. If a collar is used, bring it up behind the head and under the jaw for better control. A walk should be a pleasure for both parties and is very easy to accomplish if you keep things under control. If you're having trouble with a controlled walk, seek help from a trainer. It will only take a few lessons, and with proper instructions, you'll be in charge of the leisurely walk. Your dog wants leadership and guidance from you as the pack leader, so don't feel guilty about being tough.

If your walks are in a neighborhood with many other furry friends, always carry some mace or a small squirt gun with ammonia in it to spray if a dog argument should arise. Never run! Turn and face the charging dog with a powerful stance, scream at it, and use your mace or squirt gun (must be super soaker size). Knowing the area and the dogs where you walk is wise. Most people try to keep their dogs under control, but on occasion, one will burst out the front door and head right for you. Pre-plan a course of action in your mind of what you would do if this should happen. If two large dogs tangle, you could get terribly injured. That's where the mace would save you and your dog.

You also need to school your young children on the safety of walking if a dog should charge at them. Go walking with your kids and teach them the safe streets to enjoy when walking with the dog. Wear a reflective vest if walking after dark. Stores have wonderful blinkers to put on the dog's collar as well as many reflective collars.

Play it safe and enjoy this wonderful interaction with your furry buddy.

See – Collars, Harness, Identification Tags, Jogging, and Leashes

Warts - Pretty, pretty, pretty. Warts are very common in all dogs as they age. They can start showing up around seven years of age, and if caught early, some vets laser them off. Cockers and Poodles can be big wart producers, but any or all dogs usually end up with a few of these beauty marks. With time, warts can get as large as a nickel and have a waxy substance around them or even weep, so it's a good idea to keep the hair short around the wart for cleanliness. Warts can become an irritant to the dog and may have to be removed, but don't worry: another one will take its place. They aren't anything to worry about as far as your pet's health goes, but they can become quite a challenge for your groomer to maneuver around.

Washing - *See Bathe, Grooming, and Shampoo*

Water Bowls - Just a reminder to always have plenty of fresh water available for our best friend, and don't forget to raise the bowls up if you have a large dog or one with a neck/back problem. Also, get a heated bowl for those pets kept outside during the winter. One tablespoon of vinegar in the water will keep it crystal clear all of the time.
See- Stainless Steel Bowls

Water Drinkers - What goes in must come out. Pay attention to the amount of water your pooch consumes. I guarantee you will notice when the amount is excessive. A signal of too much water for a puppy is when it constantly runs to the water bowl and drinks. Just because it is young does not mean a problem isn't present. Many pups have bad kidneys from birth—excessive drinking is a clue to have your vet run blood tests to check kidney function. If you have paid a large amount of money for your dog, most breeders will be very willing to replace the puppy for a healthy one. This may mean that two pups will be running the house for a while if you have become attached to the original one. It's also vital to get your ill pup on a recommended food to help with kidney function, so be on top of this. Kidney failure is probably the number one organ problem your dog will struggle with as it ages, and noticeable intake of water is a good reason to get it tested. The urine usually will be very clear due to water consumption.

This is a good time for a check-up at the clinic, and also to buy a shop vac.

Cushing's disease and diabetes also create excessive water intake. Diabetes usually happens around seven years of age and Cushing's is around nine years of age. All of these most common excessive water issues require medical attention, so visit your vet.

See - Excessive Thirst

Wee Wee Wrap - A wrap is a garment that can be purchased in pet stores and catalogs to wrap around the mid-section of your male dog to prevent lifting of legs and to help with incontinence. You can also make your own. Measure your dog's mid-section to get the proper size and fit. These gadgets are wonderful and should be used when you take your dog to other people's homes or in your own home.

You might find it helpful to insert a portion of a diaper on the wrap before placing it onto your dog. This will help with absorption of the urine.

See – Incontinence and Leg Lifters

Welts - Welts are when your dog's skin becomes raised, usually the size of a dime, and red and itchy. The cause is an allergic reaction to something. These welts can cover the dog's body or be limited to a certain area. They can remain an irritant for twelve to twenty-four hours and leave as fast as they come, but don't hesitate to call the vet for advice. Vets usually encourage using Benadryl, but make sure to check on the amount.

See – Allergies, Itch, Scratching, and
Seasonal Allergies

Worms - This subject is so large I would probably lose your attention if I described them all. I want to stress the importance of a worm-free dog for the dog's health and yours. Checking its stool at least yearly is a must. If you give heartworm medicine, it also covers three or four other parasites the dog could pick up, which is great. However, some of these worms can be very difficult to get rid of and can raise havoc with the dog's system, causing runny or bloody stool, bloating, etc.

If you get a new puppy or adopt an older dog, I suggest checking for worms by taking a stool sample to your vet first. Some types of parasites are very contagious and spread through the soil, even if you scoop poop, so be very cautious. If you live in a Southern state, the likelihood of contracting a parasite is much higher due to the warmer weather, so stay on top of it.

Many types of worms cannot be seen by the naked eye in your dog's droppings, so you will need to have a stool sample tested. But tapeworm is very visible in the stool and looks like little white pieces of rice. These little segments break off the mother ship and travel out through the rectum, usually dying in the hair around the rectal area. If you notice this, contact your vet. Most of the supply stores also carry tapeworm medications; just follow the amount according to the weight of your dog.

Dogs that go to boarding kennels, doggie daycare, or an area where there is a high volume of dogs going number two are at a much higher risk of picking up parasites than those kept at home. Hunting dogs can also be at a higher risk due to contact with animal feces or innards. Heartworm is quite different and is checked through the blood.

See – Heartworm and Tapeworm

Xtra Hugs, Xtra Love, Xtra Patience, Xtra Trust

*"Xhilaration"- the feeling you get
when your pooch has finally got it.*

Xtra Hugs, Xtra Love, Xtra Patience, Xtra Trust . . .

"You" - the person your dog
ultimately looks to for love, guidance, patience, and kisses.

Yards - Our yards can become a big playpen for our dogs, a sort of worry-free area they can roam around in to get exercise. We, the humans, are responsible for keeping our pets in our own yard out of respect for those we live around. However, many subdivisions do not allow fencing, so an underground fence or tie-out is what you need to protect and control your pet. In this case, the underground fence is my choice because it allows the dog more freedom in its own yard. If you can put a fence up, do it, and you'll love it as much as your dog. Make sure it is escape-free so your pooch cannot go under, over, or through a hole. There are spring hinges for gates so they close automatically.

If you have a young dog or puppy, be sure to take the time to monitor its behavior in the yard for a while, stopping bad habits of digging and eating stones or wood. Cleaning your yard of droppings is also very important. This should be a daily habit to keep the yard clean for yourself and your dog. Burn marks from urine can upset you turf lovers, so try the pills available at most stores that carry dog supplies. This pill neutralizes the urine, eliminating the burning aspect so you have a lovely looking yard.

Many of us enjoy feeding the birds in a fenced in yard, but think about moving the feeder outside the fence. This stops the dog from getting into the bird poop and having encounters with raccoons, squirrels, skunks, rabbits, or whatever other creature makes bird seed its dinner. These creatures of the earth may be cute, but they carry parasites that can affect your dog.

Let's not forget those fleas and ticks too. Your local gardening center or pet store should supply a spray or crystal to put on the lawn to control these annoying bugs.

Last, please teach your pet good yard manners. Respect your neighbors by not allowing annoying and excessive barking, especially if you're in a close-knit neighborhood. If you give respect, you'll receive it back.

> See - Deck, Electric Fence, Fencing the
> Yard, Fleas, Identification Tags, and
> Raccoons

Yawning - Have you ever known why your dog yawns? It's very interesting to watch what causes your dog to yawn. It will perform as we do, spreading those lips and showing us its pearly whites when it's tired, bored, or relaxed. However, yawning can also appear when your dog is stressed, nervous, or afraid. Big yawns along with whimpers are Fido's way of trying to chill out on its own and relieve the anxiety. So pay attention and I bet if you watch your dog yawn, it will make you yawn too.

Yeast Infections - This is a common skin eruption in many types of dogs. Itchy, smelly, black-looking skin, crusty patches, very red and infected ears, eyes, feet, and rectal area with discolored brownish hair are all signs of yeast infections. That may be long-winded, but it's the truth.

What can you do? This tends to be food or system related, so first no foods with grains in them (this means treats too). You must stick to it or don't bother, so absolutely no cheating. I'm going to give you a name of a website that can do wonders for some dogs I have known: Nzymes.com. Remember, you the owner are the most important component of helping your pet. This is an agonizing issue for your dog and for you, but I believe if you are strict with a diet and seek help from the above site, great improvements can happen. The grain-free food may be pricier than standard food, but you must consider the cost of a vet bill in your quest for a non-itchy, non-smelly dog.

Treating the areas affected with any antifungal product that we humans use from the drug store is very helpful. I recommend applying this cream to the ears, body, rectal area, and between the toes twice a day. Again, these creams are found in the athlete's foot department of any pharmacy. Here are some brands I mentioned in other articles in this book: Lotrimin AF, Lamisil, and Monistat are all great. Try different brands until you figure out which one works best for your dog. A reminder here to always keep an eye on your pet for about ten minutes after you apply this cream so it doesn't just go and lick it off. This time will allow the skin to absorb the cream. Otherwise it's a waste of time. You may want to put a cone on for a short while to let the cream penetrate.

See – Allergies, Blackened Skin, Cones, Discolored Hair, Digging, Eczema, Feet Licker, Fungus, and Scratching

Yogurt - This food product is your friend if your dog has loose stool or irritable bowel issues. Use an organic yogurt that contains the natural bacteria, vanilla flavored or plain. You can give this a couple times a day: 1/4 cup for small dogs, 1/3 cup for medium dogs, and 1/2 cup for large dogs. They usually love it too. Yogurt is a great additive to the daily feeding, if you so choose.

See - Diarrhea and Soft Stool

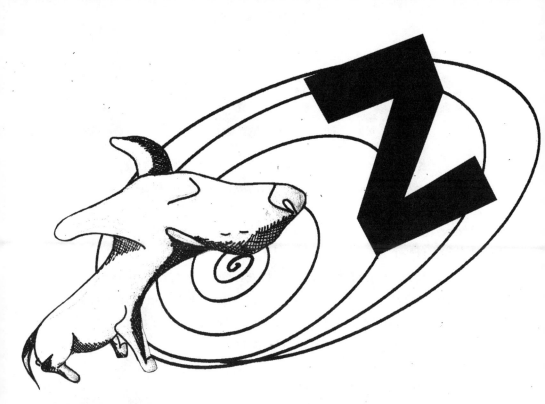

"Zenith" - the pinnacle of your relationship
with your dog when training is complete.

Zest and Zing - Be sure to keep the zest and zing in your pet's life; after all, what puts the zest back into your life more than man's best friend? If you're down, depressed, or lonely, consider adopting, buying, or borrowing one of these wonderful creatures. You'll feel your body come back to life with all the love and laughter you get.

Zits - Yes, dogs get zits too.
> *See – Acne, Pimples, and Stainless Steel*
> *Bowls*

Zone – Do you know how often your dog is in the "Zone"? If it lives in a balanced environment, the answer would be 100% of the time. However, if your household is one filled with stress and hectic conditions, your family pet absorbs all the energy and becomes what its surroundings dictate. Your pet feels all the worry, fear, and anxiety you emit and send out into the atmosphere. So "chill out" and get in the Zone where your dog lives naturally.

<u>Poisons</u>

Animal Poison Control Center 1-888-426-4435 or 1-900-680-0000

People Foods That Are Toxic:
Advil
Artificial sweetener containing xylitol
Aspirin containing acetylsalicylic acid (ASA)
Chocolate
Cocoa
Coffee
Grapes
Ibuprofen
Mushrooms
Naproxen
Onion
Painkillers such as Metacam with ASA
Raisins
Shellfish
Sudafed
Tylenol

Deadly Chemicals:
Antifreeze
Battery Acid
Bleach
Carbolic Acid
Drain Cleaner
Fertilizer
Glue
Household Cleansers

Insecticides
Kerosene
Laundry Detergent
Motor Oil
Nail Polish Remover
Paint Brush Cleaner
Paint Thinner
Pine Cleaner
Plaster
Putty
Sidewalk Salt
Turpentine

Poisonous Flowers:
Amaryllis
Buttercup
Calla Lilly
Christmas Rose
Chrysanthemum
Crocus
Daffodil (Bulb)
Easter Lily
Foxglove
Hyacinth (Bulb)
Iris (Root)
Jessamine
Morning Glory
Narcissus
Peony
Periwinkle
Poinsettia

Primrose
Tulip (Bulb)

Houseplants:

Aloe Vera
Asparagus Fern
Caladium
Colocasia (Elephant Ear)
Dieffenbachia (Dumb Cane)
Mistletoe
Mum
Philodendron
Poinsettia
Umbrella Plant

"Somedays you're the

D O G

Somedays you're the

HYDRANT"

THANK YOU!

DISCLAIMER

The author does not intend to nor does she provide medical advice for any pet or pet owner. She does not make any claims or assertions that she has medical training and/or degrees, nor does she have any specialized courses in animal care or training. The author only provides helpful hints that she has accrued through her many years of caring for and grooming animals. The author understands, as should the reader, each animal/pet is unique and special, and that treatment for routine maintenance, serious and life-threatening medical issues should be sought from a veterinarian. Further, it is not the intent of the author that any person reading this book should solely rely on the contents herein for the care and maintenance of the animal/pet. If professional advice and guidance is required, the reader should seek such professional, medical advice forthwith. Finally, the author does not guarantee or warrant any information provided in this book; the information is conveyed only as useful tips to be utilized by pet owners as he/she sees fit and appropriate.

QUICK TIPS

A dog's temperature is 101° or 102°

Cut nails monthly

Scoop your poop

Let the dog's energy work with you

Clean water daily

Always carry a spare leash

Don't overfeed

Bathe your dog regularly

Kenneling is good

No chocolates

Keep the rear end free and clear

Be diligent about potty training

Make sure the collar fits properly

Know your dog's anxieties

Brush your dog's teeth

Always keep a First Aid Kit on hand

Savings Account for your dog

Keep your dog cool in the summer

Keep your dog warm in the winter

 Keep your vaccines up to date

 Toys are fun for dogs too

 Laugh with your dog

 Take pictures of your dog

Enhance your life with your dog

No shellfish

Supply a comfortable bed

 Control the digging

DOG SAYINGS AND PROVERBS

* A house is not a home without a dog.

* Dog's are people with short legs and fur coats.

* "A good dog deserves a good bone." – US proverb

* Husband and dog missing. . . 25¢ reward for dog.

* If you want the best seat in the house . . . move your dog.

* "To live long, eat like a cat, and drink like a dog." – German proverb

* Recycle bones here.

* Chasing your tail gets you no where . . . 'cept back to where you started.

* "One dog barks at something, the rest bark at him." – Chinese proverb

* Barking dog never bites.

* Let sleeping dogs lie.

* "Those who sleep with dogs will rise with fleas." - Italian proverb

* Life is just one table scrap after another.

* A house is not a home without a dog.

* "Only mad dogs and Englishmen go out in the noonday sun." – Indian proverb

* In dog years I'm dead.

NOTES